*1971*

# PLATO'S *MENO:*

## Text and Criticism

# WADSWORTH STUDIES IN PHILOSOPHICAL CRITICISM
*Alexander Sesonske, General Editor*

## HUMAN UNDERSTANDING:
### Studies in the Philosophy of David Hume

## META-*MEDITATIONS*:
### Studies in Descartes

## PLATO'S *MENO*:
### Text and Criticism

## PLATO'S *REPUBLIC*:
### Interpretation and Criticism

## LIMITS OF LIBERTY:
### Studies of Mill's *On Liberty*

## ARISTOTLE'S *ETHICS*:
### Issues and Interpretations

# PLATO'S *MENO:*

## Text and Criticism

*edited by*
*Alexander Sesonske and Noel Fleming*
UNIVERSITY OF CALIFORNIA, SANTA BARBARA

*Wadsworth Publishing Company, Inc.*
BELMONT, CALIFORNIA

# WADSWORTH STUDIES IN PHILOSOPHICAL CRITICISM

The idea of a series of Studies in Philosophical Criticism developed in response to a growing problem in American universities. Philosophy can be taught most successfully in small classes; philosophical understanding grows in the course of a dialogue where problems are discussed from diverse points of view by men who differ in experience and temperament. But with the increase in college enrollments, the size of introductory classes has grown larger and the possibility of a dialogue between professor and students more remote. Our hope is that the Studies in Philosophical Criticism will make a dialogue of sorts possible in a class of a hundred, or a thousand, as well as in smaller classes and seminars. Each volume in the series contains a collection of critical writings related to a single classical philosophical text, such as Descartes' *Meditations* or Plato's *Republic*. These critical writings are not substitutes for the classical work, but supplements to it. They should be read in conjunction with the classical text. So used, they will bring to bear on the problems raised by Descartes, Hume, or Plato that diversity of voices and viewpoints which is the heart of the dialogue—and also, we hope, will prompt the student to add his voice to the discussion.

In selecting material for the volumes in the series, the editors have not searched primarily for writings which provide a definitive analysis of the classical text, but have rather selected those papers they thought might be most useful in undergraduate courses in philosophy, both to provoke students into serious engagement with the text and the problems found there, and to present them with a variety of philosophical styles and idioms. Most of the writings reprinted are quite contemporary; they were selected not only for their excellence but also as an indication that many of the classical problems of philosophy persist as centers of current controversy. We believe this format also achieves one prime desideratum: it acquaints the student with both the great works of the philosophical tradition and the most contemporary concepts, techniques, and modes of thought.

# CONTENTS

# PLATO'S *MENO:*
## Text and Criticism

# INTRODUCTION

It has often been said that the best introduction to philosophy is through Plato, and many feel that the best introduction to Plato is through his earlier dialogues, of which the *Meno* is an excellent and mature example. Socrates wrote nothing himself, but talked at length to the young men of Athens, including Plato; most scholars now agree that in his earlier dialogues Plato gives us a rather accurate picture of Socrates and the questioning, inconclusive, ironical method of philosophizing which he so powerfully employed.

The line between Socrates and Plato, who was perhaps the greatest of all philosophers and indisputably the founder of the Western philosophical tradition, is hard, if not impossible, to find. In the *Meno* we have the first clear indications of some positions now generally regarded as characteristically Platonic rather than Socratic; for example, the view that knowledge is recollection. For the philosopher, however, and certainly for the beginning student, the question of what was original with Plato and what belongs to Socrates is of little importance. What is important is that the *Meno* is a philosophically rich dialogue written by Plato, in which we find not only philosophical problems and ideas, but also a master philosopher, Socrates, talking and acting very much as did the historical Socrates some 2400 years ago, when Plato was a young man listening to him in the streets and gathering places of Athens.

One further point about the life of Socrates is worth noting. Late in the *Meno* there are explicit references to the accusation brought against Socrates, which led to his trial and execution in 399 B.C. The *Meno* is thus the first (in dramatic order, though probably not chronologically) of the series of dialogues that portray the last days of Socrates. The others are the *Euthyphro*, with Socrates on his way to court; the *Apology*, Socrates' speech defending himself at the trial; the *Crito*, in which Socrates, in prison awaiting execution, considers whether he should escape as his friends and pupils urge; and finally, the *Phaedo*, which—after a lengthy discussion of the immortality of the soul—ends with the death of Socrates. So we must understand that Socrates is not merely playing an intellectual game when we encounter him in the *Meno*, but actually risking his life in the kind of conversa-

**1**

tion we find portrayed. This conviction—that the pursuit of truth is worth the risk of one's life—is one of Socrates' major contributions to the Western tradition. He believed that philosophy must be *lived*, not merely thought about or verbally accepted; for its value lies in its contribution to the goodness of a man's life. His own life is our best exemplification of this view.

Many of Plato's early dialogues are short and inconclusive, and follow a rather similar pattern. First, within an ordinary conversation, Socrates raises a question of definition: *What is courage, or friendship, or piety?* The participants then propose various answers, which are shown to be unsatisfactory. The dialogue ends with the participants not knowing just what to say next, but admitting that they have not answered the question. The *Meno* differs from these earlier dialogues in that it continues long after the point at which they would have stopped, and the argument becomes much more complex. It is this that makes it so valuable as an introduction to philosophy. For, after the central and original question about a moral concept has been explored, and Meno no longer knows what to say, Plato turns the dialogue to an explicit examination of questions of a quite different sort—questions about the nature of knowledge and the methods by which it may be attained. This explicit shift to logical, methodological, and metaphysical questions opens the road to the whole of Plato's later thought and presents us, in the *Meno*, with a wealth of material for discussion and exploration.

The critical articles we have gathered here reflect the complexity of the *Meno*. The first two are concerned with questions closely related to Socrates' quest for moral knowledge in the early dialogues. Beginning with Meno's question "Can virtue be taught?"—that is, can excellence of character be imparted to a man by a deliberate process of teaching, can instruction make men good?—F. J. E. Woodbridge discusses several questions about the moral influence of education. These questions were of great importance to Plato and are of major significance today: What are the limits of education? Does education in a formal discipline, such as geometry, have any effect on a man's life or character? Is knowledge of geometry related in any way to our knowledge of good and evil? If virtue cannot be taught, can education still contribute in some indirect way to the shaping of a desirable character? These are not merely academic questions; the *Meno* and Woodbridge's discussion should make us more clearly aware of their import and more wary of some current dogmas concerning education.

The second article, by Gerasimos Santas, discusses another moral concept: the puzzling Socratic contention (found in many of the early dialogues, including the *Meno*) that no man voluntarily pursues evil things or performs unjust actions. The doctrine is puzzling because it seems to conflict with our frequent experience that men do voluntarily, even deliberately, harm themselves and others. Santas calls this doctrine the Socratic paradox; he then proceeds to argue that Socrates espouses not one, but two distinct doctrines, and that, if these doctrines are properly understood, the air of paradox disappears. His article is a good example of contemporary critical method in philosophy. Paying careful attention to exactly what Plato says and the context in which it is said, he makes clear distinctions, which unravel ambiguities in the text; and he remains attentive to logical and linguistic nuances that may furnish insights into meaning. The underlying problem here is the same as that of the Woodbridge article, the problem of the relation of knowledge to conduct. This is perhaps the central problem in all of Plato's early writings, a problem made explicit in the *Meno* when the familiar Socratic doctrine "Virtue is knowledge" is first defended, then rejected.

In the third article, Richard Robinson's "Socratic Definition," we turn from the moral to the logical questions raised in the *Meno*. The *Meno* is the first dialogue in which Plato discusses at some length the logical questions implicit in the Socratic method. Socrates asked for definitions; now Plato asks, "What is a definition?" Just what sort of a question is "What is virtue?" and what sort of answer would suffice? Robinson's discussion of the quest for definition in the early dialogues should aid our understanding of logic and language as well as of Plato.

Bernard Phillips' "The Significance of Meno's Paradox" carries us from the logical to the metaphysical level of the *Meno*. Midway in the dialogue, Meno raises an objection to the whole Socratic mode of inquiry. Phillips sees this objection as a crucial test of Plato's developing philosophy; as an empiricist challenge to Plato's belief that reality is to be apprehended by thought, not sensation. Phillips, then, finds in the *Meno* the confrontation of empiricism and rationalism, which has been the major division in the history of philosophy.

The last two articles in our collection are more general. Alexander Sesonske, in "Knowing and Saying," tries to give a coherent account of the series of "digressions" that constitute such a large part of the *Meno*, and shows how they might have all grown out of the assumption underlying the Socratic method—that we can achieve knowledge by talking. Taking the relation of knowledge to speech as a clue to understanding the dialogue, Sesonske succeeds, perhaps, in provoking us into attending to this important and puzzling relation. R. M. Hare's "Philosophical Discoveries" begins with a discussion of the current tendency to transform metaphysical questions into problems about language and then turns to the *Meno*. This article is *not* a criticism of the *Meno* at all, but rather a discussion of a contemporary philosophical problem, the problem of the nature of philosophical analysis. Hare reveals that Plato, in the *Meno*, was also concerned with this problem and that the solution Plato suggests there is worth considering seriously even now. Thus, the inclusion of this paper in our collection serves several purposes: it provides a transition from ancient Greek philosophy to contemporary philosophical thought; it shows that contemporary philosophers, not directly concerned with problems in the history of philosophy, may yet contribute to our understanding of historical writings; and it very clearly shows that the philosophy of Plato is still relevant to current problems.

A.S.
N.F.

# MENO*

## *Plato*

### Persons of the Dialogue

MENO     A SLAVE OF MENO

SOCRATES     ANYTUS

*Meno.* CAN you tell me, Socrates, whether virtue is acquired by teaching or by practice; or if neither by teaching nor practice, then whether it comes to man by nature, or in what other way?

*Socrates.* O Meno, there was a time when the Thessalians were famous among the other Hellenes only for their riches and their riding; but now, if I am not mistaken, they are equally famous for their wisdom, especially at Larisa, which is the native city of your friend Aristippus. And this is Gorgias' doing; for when he came there, the flower of the Aleuadae, among them your admirer Aristippus, and the other chiefs of the Thessalians, fell in love with his wisdom. And he has taught you the habit of answering questions in a grand and bold style, which becomes those who know, and is the style in which he himself answers all comers; and any Hellene who likes may ask him anything. How different is our lot! my dear Meno. Here at Athens 71 there is a dearth of the commodity, and all wisdom seems to have emigrated from us to you. I am certain that if you were to ask any Athenian whether virtue was natural or acquired, he would laugh in your face, and say: "Stranger, you have far too good an opinion of me, if you think that I can answer your question. For I literally do not know what virtue is, and much less whether it is acquired by teaching or not." And I myself, Meno, living as I do in this region of poverty, am as poor as the rest of the world; and I confess with shame that I know literally nothing about virtue; and when I do not know the "quid" of anything how can I know the "quale"? How, if I knew nothing at all of Meno, could I tell if he was fair, or the opposite of fair; rich and noble, or the reverse of rich and noble? Do you think that I could?

* From *The Dialogues of Plato*, translated by B. Jowett (1892).

*Men.* No, indeed. But are you in earnest, Socrates, in saying that you do not know what virtue is? And am I to carry back this report of you to Thessaly?

*Soc.* Not only that, my dear boy, but you may say further that I have never known of anyone else who did, in my judgment.

*Men.* Then you have never met Gorgias when he was at Athens?

*Soc.* Yes, I have.

*Men.* And did you not think that he knew?

*Soc.* I have not a good memory, Meno, and therefore I cannot now tell what I thought of him at the time. And I dare say that he did know, and that you know what he said: please, therefore, to remind me of what he said; or, if you would rather, tell me your own view; for I suspect that you and he think much alike.

*Men.* Very true.

*Soc.* Then, as he is not here, never mind him, and do you tell me: By the gods, Meno, be generous, and tell me what you say that virtue is; for I shall be truly delighted to find that I have been mistaken, and that you and Gorgias do really have this knowledge; although I have been just saying that I have never found anybody who had.

*Men.* There will be no difficulty, Socrates, in answering your question. Let us take first the virtue of a man—he should know how to administer the state, and in the administration of it to benefit his friends and harm his enemies; and he must also be careful not to suffer harm himself. A woman's virtue, if you wish to know about that, may also be easily described: her duty is to order her house, and keep what is indoors, and obey her husband. Every age, every condition of life, young or old, male or female, bond or free, has a different virtue: 72 there are virtues numberless, and no lack of definitions of them; for virtue is relative to the actions and ages of each of us in all that we do. And the same may be said of vice, Socrates.

*Soc.* How fortunate I am, Meno! When I ask you for one virtue, you present me with a swarm of them, which are in your keeping. Suppose that I carry on the figure of the swarm, and ask of you, What is the nature of the bee? and you answer that there are many kinds of bees, and I reply: But do bees differ as bees, because there are many and different kinds of them; or are they not rather to be distinguished by some other quality, as, for example, beauty, size, or shape? How would you answer me?

*Men.* I should answer that bees do not differ from one another, as bees.

*Soc.* And if I went on to say: That is what I desire to know, Meno; tell me what is the quality in which they do not differ, but are all alike;—would you be able to answer?

*Men.* I should.

*Soc.* And so of the virtues, however many and different they may be, they have all a common nature which makes them virtues; and on this he who would answer the question, "What is virtue?" would do well to have his eye fixed: Do you understand?

*Men.* I am beginning to understand; but I do not as yet take hold of the question as I could wish.

*Soc.* When you say, Meno, that there is one virtue of a man, another of a woman, another of a child, and so on, does this apply only to virtue, or would you say the same of health, and size, and strength? Or is the nature of health always the same, whether in man or woman?

*Men.* I should say that health is the same, both in man and woman.

*Soc.* And is not this true of size and strength? If a woman is strong, she will be strong by reason of the same form and of the same strength subsisting in her which there is in the man. I mean to say that strength, as strength, whether of man or woman, is the same. Is there any difference?

*Men.* I think not.

*Soc.* And will not virtue, as virtue, be the same, whether in a 73 child or in a grown-up person, in a woman or in a man?

*Men.* I cannot help feeling, Socrates, that this case is different from the others.

*Soc.* But why? Were you not saying that the virtue of a man was to order a state, and the virtue of a woman was to order a house?

*Men.* I did say so.

*Soc.* And can either house or state or anything be well ordered without temperance and without justice?

*Men.* Certainly not.

*Soc.* Then they who order a state or a house temperately or justly order them with temperance and justice?

*Men.* Certainly.

*Soc.* Then both men and women, if they are to be good men and women, must have the same virtues of temperance and justice?

*Men.* True.

*Soc.* And can either a young man or an elder one be good, if they are intemperate and unjust?

*Men.* They cannot.

*Soc.* They must be temperate and just?

*Men.* Yes.

*Soc.* Then all men are good in the same way, and by participation in the same virtues?

*Men.* Such is the inference.

*Soc.* And they surely would not have been good in the same way, unless their virtue had been the same?

*Men.* They would not.

*Soc.* Then now that the sameness of all virtue has been proven, try and remember what you and Gorgias say that virtue is.

*Men.* Will you have one definition of them all?

*Soc.* That is what I am seeking.

*Men.* If you want to have one definition of them all, I know not what to say, but that virtue is the power of governing mankind.

*Soc.* And does this definition of virtue include all virtue? Is virtue the same in a child and a slave, Meno? Can the child govern his father, or the slave his master; and would he who governed be any longer a slave?

*Men.* I think not, Socrates.

*Soc.* No, indeed; there would be small reason in that. Yet once more, fair friend; according to you, virtue is "the power of governing"; but do you not add "justly and not unjustly"?

*Men.* Yes, Socrates; I agree there; for justice is virtue.

*Soc.* Would you say "virtue," Meno, or "a virtue"?

*Men.* What do you mean?

*Soc.* I mean as I might say about anything; that a round, for example, is "a figure" and not simply "figure," and I should adopt this mode of speaking, because there are other figures.

*Men.* Quite right; and that is just what I am saying about virtue—that there are other virtues as well as justice.

74     *Soc.* What are they? tell me the names of them, as I would tell you the names of the other figures if you asked me.

*Men.* Courage and temperance and wisdom and magnanimity are virtues; and there are many others.

*Soc.* Yes, Meno; and again we are in the same case: in searching after one virtue we have found many, though not in the same way as before; but we have been unable to find the common virtue which runs through them all.

*Men.* Why, Socrates, even now I am not able to follow you in the attempt to get at one common notion of virtue as of other things.

*Soc.* No wonder; but I will try to get nearer if I can, for you know that all things have a common notion. Suppose now that some one asked you the question which I asked before: Meno, he would say, what is figure? And if you answered "roundness," he would reply to you, in my way of speaking, by asking whether you would say that roundness is "figure" or "a figure"; and you would answer "a figure."

*Men.* Certainly.

*Soc.* And for this reason—that there are other figures?

*Men.* Yes.

*Soc.* And if he proceeded to ask, What other figures are there? you would have told him.

*Men.* I should.

*Soc.* And if he similarly asked what colour is, and you answered whiteness, and the questioner rejoined, Would you say that whiteness is colour or a colour? you would reply, A colour, because there are other colours as well.

*Men.* I should.

*Soc.* And if he had said, Tell me what they are?—you would have told him of other colours which are colours just as much as whiteness.

*Men.* Yes.

*Soc.* And suppose that he were to pursue the matter in my way, he would say: Ever and anon we are landed in particulars, but this is not what I want; tell me then, since you call them by a common name, and say that they are all figures, even when opposed to one another, what is that common nature which you designate as figure—which contains straight as well as round, and is no more one than the other— that would be your mode of speaking?

*Men.* Yes.

*Soc.* And in speaking thus, you do not mean to say that the round is not round any more than straight, or the straight not any more straight than round?

*Men.* Certainly not.

*Soc.* You only assert that the round figure is not more a figure than the straight, or the straight than the round?

*Men.* Very true.

*Soc.* To what then do we give the name of figure? Try and answer. Suppose that when a person asked you this question either about figure or colour, you were to reply, Man, I do not understand what you want, or know what you are saying; he would look rather 75 astonished and say: Do you not understand that I am looking for the "simile in multis"? And then he might put the question in another form: Meno, he might say, what is that "simile in multis" which you call figure, and which includes not only round and straight figures, but all? Could you not answer that question, Meno? I wish that you would try; the attempt will be good practice with a view to the answer about virtue.

*Men.* I would rather that you should answer, Socrates.

*Soc.* Shall I indulge you?

*Men.* By all means.

*Soc.* And then you will tell me about virtue?

*Men.* I will.

*Soc.* Then I must do my best, for there is a prize to be won.

*Men.* Certainly.

*Soc.* Well, I will try and explain to you what figure is. What do you say to this answer?—Figure is the only thing which always follows colour. Will you be satisfied with it, as I am sure that I should be, if you would let me have a similar definition of virtue?

*Men.* But, Socrates, it is such a simple answer.

*Soc.* Why simple?

*Men.* Because, according to you, figure is that which always follows colour.

(*Soc.* Granted.)

*Men.* But if a person were to say that he does not know what colour is, any more than what figure is—what sort of answer would you have given him?

*Soc.* I should have told him the truth. And if he were a philosopher of the eristic and antagonistic sort, I should say to him: You have my answer, and if I am wrong, your business is to take up the argument and refute me. But if we were friends, and were talking as you and I are now, I should reply in a milder strain and more in the dialectician's vein; that is to say, I should not only speak the truth, but I should make use of premisses which the person interrogated would be willing to admit. And this is the way in which I shall endeavour to approach you. You will acknowledge, will you not, that there is such a thing as an end, or termination, or extremity?—all which words I use in the same sense, although I am aware that Prodicus might draw distinctions about them: but still you, I am sure, would speak of a thing as ended or terminated—that is all which I am saying—not anything very difficult.

*Men.* Yes, I should; and I believe that I understand your meaning.

*Soc.* And you would speak of a surface and also of a solid, as for 76 example in geometry.

*Men.* Yes.

*Soc.* Well then, you are now in a condition to understand my definition of figure. I define figure to be that in which the solid ends; or, more concisely, the limit of solid.

*Men.* And now, Socrates, what is colour?

*Soc.* You are outrageous, Meno, in thus plaguing a poor old man to give you an answer, when you will not take the trouble of remembering what is Gorgias' definition of virtue.

*Men.* When you have told me what I ask, I will tell you, Socrates.

*Soc.* A man who was blindfolded has only to hear you talking, and he would know that you are a fair creature and have still many lovers.

*Men.* Why do you think so?

*Soc.* Why, because you always speak in imperatives: like all beauties when they are in their prime, you are tyrannical; and also, as I suspect, you have found out that I have a weakness for the fair, and therefore to humour you I must answer.

*Men.* Please do.

*Soc.* Would you like me to answer you after the manner of Gorgias, which is familiar to you?

*Men.* I should like nothing better.

*Soc.* Do not he and you and Empedocles say that there are certain effluences of existence?

*Men.* Certainly.

*Soc.* And passages into which and through which the effluences pass?

*Men.* Exactly.

*Soc.* And some of the effluences fit into the passages, and some of them are too small or too large?

*Men.* True.

*Soc.* And there is such a thing as sight?

*Men.* Yes.

*Soc.* And now, as Pindar says, "read my meaning":—colour is an effluence of form, commensurate with sight, and palpable to sense.

*Men.* That, Socrates, appears to me to be an admirable answer.

*Soc.* Why, yes, because it happens to be one which you have been in the habit of hearing: and your wit will have discovered, I suspect, that you may explain in the same way the nature of sound and smell, and of many other similar phenomena.

*Men.* Quite true.

*Soc.* The answer, Meno, was in the orthodox solemn vein, and therefore was more acceptable to you than the other answer about figure.

*Men.* Yes.

*Soc.* And yet, O son of Alexidemus, I cannot help thinking that the other was the better; and I am sure that you would be of the same opinion, if you would only stay and be initiated, and were not compelled, as you said yesterday, to go away before the mysteries.

*Men.* But I will stay, Socrates, if you will give me many such
77 answers.

*Soc.* Well then, for my own sake as well as for yours, I will do my very best; but I am afraid that I shall not be able to give you very many as good: and now, in your turn, you are to fulfil your promise, and tell me what virtue is in the universal; and do not make a singular into a plural, as the facetious say of those who break a thing, but deliver virtue to me whole and sound, and not broken into a number of pieces: I have given you the pattern.

*Men.* Well then, Socrates, virtue, as I take it, is when he, who desires the honourable, is able to provide it for himself; so the poet says, and I say too—

Virtue is the desire of things honourable and the power of attaining them.

*Soc.* And does he who desires the honourable also desire the good?

*Men.* Certainly.

*Soc.* Then are there some who desire the evil and others who desire the good? Do not all men, my dear sir, desire good?

*Men.* I think not.

*Soc.* There are some who desire evil?

*Men.* Yes.

*Soc.* Do you mean that they think the evils which they desire, to be good; or do they know that they are evil and yet desire them?

*Men.* Both, I think.

*Soc.* And do you really imagine, Meno, that a man knows evils to be evils and desires them notwithstanding?

*Men.* Certainly I do.

*Soc.* And desire is of possession?

*Men.* Yes, of possession.

*Soc.* And does he think that the evils will do good to him who possesses them, or does he know that they will do him harm?

*Men.* There are some who think that the evils will do them good, and others who know that they will do them harm.

*Soc.* And, in your opinion, do those who think that they will do them good know that they are evils?

*Men.* Certainly not.

*Soc.* Is it not obvious that those who are ignorant of their nature do not desire them; but they desire what they suppose to be goods although they are really evils; and if they are mistaken and suppose the evils to be goods they really desire goods?

*Men.* Yes, in that case.

*Soc.* Well, and do those who, as you say, desire evils, and think that evils are hurtful to the possessor of them, know that they will be hurt by them?

*Men.* They must know it.

*Soc.* And must they not suppose that those who are hurt are 78 miserable in proportion to the hurt which is inflicted upon them?

*Men.* How can it be otherwise?

*Soc.* But are not the miserable ill-fated?

*Men.* Yes, indeed.

*Soc.* And does any one desire to be miserable and ill-fated?

*Men.* I should say not, Socrates.

*Soc.* But if there is no one who desires to be miserable, there is no one, Meno, who desires evil; for what is misery but the desire and possession of evil?

*Men.* That appears to be the truth, Socrates, and I admit that nobody desires evil.

*Soc.* And yet, were you not saying just now that virtue is the desire and power of attaining good?

*Men.* Yes, I did say so.

*Soc.* But if this be affirmed, then the desire of good is common to all, and one man is no better than another in that respect?

*Men.* True.

*Soc.* And if one man is not better than another in desiring good, he must be better in the power of attaining it?

*Men.* Exactly.

*Soc.* Then, according to your definition, virtue would appear to be the power of attaining good?

*Men.* I entirely approve, Socrates, of the manner in which you now view this matter.

*Soc.* Then let us see whether what you say is true from another point of view; for very likely you may be right:—You affirm virtue to be the power of attaining goods?

*Men.* Yes.

*Soc.* And the goods which you mean are such as health and wealth and the possession of gold and silver, and having office and honour in the state—those are what you would call goods?

*Men.* Yes, I should include all those.

*Soc.* Then, according to Meno, who is the hereditary friend of the great king, virtue is the power of getting silver and gold; and would you add that they must be gained piously, justly, or do you deem this to be of no consequence? And is any mode of acquisition, even if unjust and dishonest, equally to be deemed virtue?

*Men.* Not virtue, Socrates, but vice.

*Soc.* Then justice or temperance or holiness, or some other part of virtue, as would appear, must accompany the acquisition, and without them the mere acquisition of good will not be virtue.

*Men.* Why, how can there be a virtue without these?

*Soc.* And the non-acquisition of gold and silver in a dishonest manner for oneself or another, or in other words the want of them, may be equally virtue?

*Men.* True.

*Soc.* Then the acquisition of such goods is no more virtue than the non-acquisition and want of them, but whatever is accompanied
79 by justice or honesty is virtue, and whatever is devoid of justice is vice.

*Men.* It cannot be otherwise, in my judgment.

*Soc.* And were we not saying just now that justice, temperance, and the like, were each of them a part of virtue?

*Men.* Yes.

*Soc.* And so, Meno, this is the way in which you mock me.

*Men.* Why do you say that, Socrates?

*Soc.* Why, because I asked you to deliver virtue into my hands whole and unbroken, and I gave you a pattern according to which you were to frame your answer; and you have forgotten already, and tell me that virtue is the power of attaining good justly, or with justice; and justice you acknowledge to be a part of virtue.

*Men.* Yes.

*Soc.* Then it follows from your own admissions, that virtue is doing what you do with a part of virtue; for justice and the like are said by you to be parts of virtue.

*Men.* What of that?

*Soc.* What of that! Why, did not I ask you to tell me the nature of virtue as a whole? And you are very far from telling me this; but declare every action to be virtue which is done with a part of virtue; as though you had told me and I must already know the whole of virtue, and this too when frittered away into little pieces. And therefore, my dear Meno, I fear that I must begin again and repeat the same question: What is virtue? For otherwise, I can only say, that every action done with a part of virtue is virtue; what else is the meaning of saying that every action done with justice is virtue? Ought I not to ask the question over again; for can any one who does not know virtue know a part of virtue?

*Men.* No; I do not say that he can.

*Soc.* Do you remember how, in the example of figure, we rejected any answer given in terms which were as yet unexplained or unadmitted?

*Men.* Yes, Socrates; and we were quite right in doing so.

*Soc.* But then, my friend, do not suppose that we can explain to any one the nature of virtue as a whole through some unexplained portion of virtue, or anything at all in that fashion; we should only have to ask over again the old question, What is virtue? Am I not right?

*Men.* I believe that you are.

*Soc.* Then begin again, and answer me, What, according to you and your friend Gorgias, is the definition of virtue?

*Men.* O Socrates, I used to be told, before I knew you, that you were always doubting yourself and making others doubt; and now 80 you are casting your spells over me, and I am simply getting bewitched and enchanted, and am at my wits' end. And if I may venture to make a jest upon you, you seem to me both in your appearance and in your power over others to be very like the flat torpedo fish, who torpifies those who come near him and touch him, as you have now torpified me, I think. For my soul and my tongue are really torpid, and I do not know how to answer you; and though I have been delivered of an infinite variety of speeches about virtue before now, and to many persons—and very good ones they were, as I thought—at this moment I cannot even say what virtue is. And I think that you are very wise in not voyaging and going away from home, for if you did in other places as you do in Athens, you would be cast into prison as a magician.

*Soc.* You are a rogue, Meno, and had all but caught me.

*Men.* What do you mean, Socrates?

*Soc.* I can tell why you made a simile about me.

*Men.* Why?

*Soc.* In order that I might make another simile about you. For I know that all pretty young gentlemen like to have pretty similes made about them—as well they may—but I shall not return the compliment. As to my being a torpedo, if the torpedo is torpid as well as the cause of torpidity in others, then indeed I am a torpedo, but not otherwise; for I perplex others, not because I am clear, but because I am utterly perplexed myself. And now I know not what virtue is, and you seem to be in the same case, although you did once perhaps know before you touched me. However, I have no objection to join with you in the enquiry.

*Men.* And how will you enquire, Socrates, into that which you do not know? What will you put forth as the subject of enquiry? And if you find what you want, how will you ever know that this is the thing which you did not know?

*Soc.* I know, Meno, what you mean; but just see what a tiresome dispute you are introducing. You argue that a man cannot enquire either about that which he knows, or about that which he does not know; for if he knows, he has no need to enquire; and if not, he cannot; for he does not know the very subject about which he is to enquire.

81        *Men.* Well, Socrates, and is not the argument sound?

*Soc.* I think not.

*Men.* Why not?

*Soc.* I will tell you why: I have heard from certain wise men and women who spoke of things divine that—

*Men.* What did they say?

*Soc.* They spoke of a glorious truth, as I conceive.

*Men.* What was it? and who were they?

*Soc.* Some of them were priests and priestesses, who had studied how they might be able to give a reason of their profession: there have been poets also, who spoke of these things by inspiration, like Pindar, and many others who were inspired. And they say—mark, now, and see whether their words are true—they say that the soul of man is immortal, and at one time has an end, which is termed dying, and at another time is born again, but is never destroyed. And the moral is, that a man ought to live always in perfect holiness. *"For in the ninth year Persephone sends the souls of those from whom she has received the penalty of ancient crime back again from beneath into the light of the sun above, and these are they who become noble kings and mighty men and great in wisdom and are called saintly heroes in after ages."* The soul, then, as being immortal, and having been born again many times, and having seen all things that exist, whether in this world or in the world below, has knowledge of them all; and it is no wonder that she should be able to call to remembrance all that she ever knew about virtue, and about everything; for as all nature is akin, and the soul has learned all things, there is no difficulty in her eliciting or as men say learning, out of a single recollection all the rest, if a man is strenuous and does not faint; for all enquiry and all learning is but recollection. And therefore we ought not to listen to this sophistical argument about the impossibility of enquiry: for it will make us idle, and is sweet only to the sluggard; but the other saying will make us active and inquisitive. In that confiding, I will gladly enquire with you into the nature of virtue.

*Men.* Yes, Socrates; but what do you mean by saying that we do not learn, and that what we call learning is only a process of recollection? Can you teach me how this is?

*Soc.* I told you, Meno, just now that you were a rogue, and now you ask whether I can teach you, when I am saying that there is no teaching, but only recollection; and thus you imagine that you will 82 involve me in a contradiction.

*Men.* Indeed, Socrates, I protest that I had no such intention. I only asked the question from habit; but if you can prove to me that what you say is true, I wish that you would.

*Soc.* It will be no easy matter, but I will try to please you to the utmost of my power. Suppose that you call one of your numerous attendants, that I may demonstrate on him.

*Men.* Certainly. Come hither, boy.

*Soc.* He is Greek, and speaks Greek, does he not?

*Men.* Yes, indeed; he was born in the house.

*Soc.* Attend now to the questions which I ask him, and observe whether he learns of me or only remembers.

*Men.* I will.

*Soc.* Tell me, boy, do you know that a figure like this is a square?

*Boy.* I do.

*Soc.* And you know that a square figure has these four lines equal?

*Boy.* Certainly.

*Soc.* And these lines which I have drawn through the middle of the square are also equal?

*Boy.* Yes.

*Soc.* A square may be of any size?

*Boy.* Certainly.

*Soc.* And if one side of the figure be of two feet, and the other side be of two feet, how much will the whole be? Let me explain: if in one direction the space was of two feet, and in the other direction of one foot, the whole would be of two feet taken once?

*Boy.* Yes.

*Soc.* But since this side is also of two feet, there are twice two feet?

*Boy.* There are.

*Soc.* Then the square is of twice two feet?

*Boy.* Yes.

*Soc.* And how many are twice two feet? count and tell me.

*Boy.* Four, Socrates.

*Soc.* And might there not be another square twice as large as this, and having like this the lines equal?

*Boy.* Yes.

*Soc.* And of how many feet will that be?

*Boy.* Of eight feet.

*Soc.* And now try and tell me the length of the line which forms the side of that double square: this is two feet—what will that be?

*Boy.* Clearly, Socrates, it will be double.

*Soc.* Do you observe, Meno, that I am not teaching the boy anything, but only asking him questions; and now he fancies that he knows how long a line is necessary in order to produce a figure of eight square feet; does he not?

*Men.* Yes.

*Soc.* And does he really know?

*Men.* Certainly not.

*Soc.* He only guesses that because the square is double, the line is double.

*Men.* True.

*Soc.* Observe him while he recalls the steps in regular order. (*To
83   the Boy.*) Tell me, boy, do you assert that a double space comes from a double line? Remember that I am not speaking of an oblong, but of a

figure equal every way, and twice the size of this—that is to say of eight feet; and I want to know whether you still say that a double square comes from a double line?

*Boy.* Yes.

*Soc.* But does not this line become doubled if we add another such line here?

*Boy.* Certainly.

*Soc.* And four such lines will make a space containing eight feet?

*Boy.* Yes.

*Soc.* Let us describe such a figure: Would you not say that this is the figure of eight feet?

*Boy.* Yes.

*Soc.* And are there not these four divisions in the figure, each of which is equal to the figure of four feet?

*Boy.* True.

*Soc.* And is not that four times four?

*Boy.* Certainly.

*Soc.* And four times is not double?

*Boy.* No, indeed.

*Soc.* But how much?

*Boy.* Four times as much.

*Soc.* Therefore the double line, boy, has given a space, not twice, but four times as much.

*Boy.* True.

*Soc.* Four times four are sixteen—are they not?

*Boy.* Yes.

*Soc.* What line would give you a space of eight feet, as this gives one of sixteen feet;—do you see?

*Boy.* Yes.

*Soc.* And the space of four feet is made from this half line?

*Boy.* Yes.

*Soc.* Good; and is not a space of eight feet twice the size of this, and half the size of the other?

*Boy.* Certainly.

*Soc.* Such a space, then, will be made out of a line greater than this one, and less than that one?

*Boy.* Yes; I think so.

*Soc.* Very good; I like to hear you say what you think. And now tell me, is not this a line of two feet and that of four?

*Boy.* Yes.

*Soc.* Then the line which forms the side of eight feet ought to be more than this line of two feet, and less than the other of four feet?

*Boy.* It ought.

*Soc.* Try and see if you can tell me how much it will be.

*Boy.* Three feet.

*Soc.* Then if we add a half to this line of two, that will be the line of three. Here are two and there is one; and on the other side, here are two also and there is one: and that makes the figure of which you speak?

*Boy.* Yes.

*Soc.* But if there are three feet this way and three feet that way, the whole space will be three times three feet?

*Boy.* That is evident.

*Soc.* And how much are three times three feet?

*Boy.* Nine.

*Soc.* And how much is the double of four?

*Boy.* Eight.

*Soc.* Then the figure of eight is not made out of a line of three?

*Boy.* No.

84    Soc. But from what line?—tell me exactly; and if you would rather not reckon, try and show me the line.

*Boy.* Indeed, Socrates, I do not know.

*Soc.* Do you see, Meno, what advances he has made in his power of recollection? He did not know at first, and he does not know now, what is the side of a figure of eight feet: but then he thought that he knew, and answered confidently as if he knew, and had no difficulty; now he has a difficulty, and neither knows nor fancies that he knows.

*Men.* True.

*Soc.* Is he not better off in knowing his ignorance?

*Men.* I think that he is.

*Soc.* If we have made him doubt, and given him the "torpedo's shock," have we done him any harm?

*Men.* I think not.

*Soc.* We have certainly, as would seem, assisted him in some degree to the discovery of the truth; and now he will wish to remedy his ignorance, but then he would have been ready to tell all the world again and again that the double space should have a double side.

*Men.* True.

*Soc.* But do you suppose that he would ever have enquired into or learned what he fancied that he knew, though he was really ignorant of it, until he had fallen into perplexity under the idea that he did not know, and had desired to know?

*Men.* I think not, Socrates.

*Soc.* Then he was the better for the torpedo's touch?

*Men.* I think so.

*Soc.* Mark now the farther development. I shall only ask him, and not teach him, and he shall share the enquiry with me: and do you watch and see if you find me telling or explaining anything to him, instead of eliciting his opinion. Tell me, boy, is not this a square of four feet which I have drawn?

*Boy.* Yes.

*Soc.* And now I add another square equal to the former one?

*Boy.* Yes.

*Soc.* And a third, which is equal to either of them?

*Boy.* Yes.

*Soc.* Suppose that we fill up the vacant corner?

*Boy.* Very good.

*Soc.* Here, then, there are four equal spaces?

*Boy.* Yes.

*Soc.* And how many times larger is this space than this other?

*Boy.* Four times.

*Soc.* But it ought to have been twice only, as you will remember.

*Boy.* True.

*Soc.* And does not this line, reaching from corner to corner, bi- 85 sect each of these spaces?

*Boy.* Yes.

*Soc.* And are there not here four equal lines which contain this space?

*Boy.* There are.

*Soc.* Look and see how much this space is.

*Boy.* I do not understand.

*Soc.* Has not each interior line cut off half of the four spaces?

*Boy.* Yes.

*Soc.* And how many spaces are there in this section?

*Boy.* Four.

*Soc.* And how many in this?

*Boy.* Two.

*Soc.* And four is how many times two?

*Boy.* Twice.

*Soc.* And this space is of how many feet?

*Boy.* Of eight feet.

*Soc.* And from what line do you get this figure?

*Boy.* From this.

*Soc.* That is, from the line which extends from corner to corner of the figure of four feet?

*Boy.* Yes.

*Soc.* And that is the line which the learned call the diagonal. And if this is the proper name, then you, Meno's slave, are prepared to affirm that the double space is the square of the diagonal?

*Boy.* Certainly, Socrates.

*Soc.* What do you say of him, Meno? Were not all these answers given out of his own head?

*Men.* Yes, they were all his own.

*Soc.* And yet, as we were just now saying, he did not know?

*Men.* True.

*Soc.* But still he had in him those notions of his—had he not?

*Men.* Yes.

*Soc.* Then he who does not know may still have true notions of that which he does not know?

*Men.* He has.

*Soc.* And at present these notions have just been stirred up in him, as in a dream; but if he were frequently asked the same questions, in different forms, he would know as well as any one at last?

*Men.* I dare say.

*Soc.* Without any one teaching him he will recover his knowledge for himself, if he is only asked questions?

*Men.* Yes.

*Soc.* And this spontaneous recovery of knowledge in him is recollection?

*Men.* True.

*Soc.* And this knowledge which he now has must he not either have acquired or always possessed?

*Men.* Yes.

*Soc.* But if he always possessed this knowledge he would always have known; or if he has acquired the knowledge he could not have acquired it in this life, unless he has been taught geometry; for he may be made to do the same with all geometry and every other branch of knowledge. Now, has any one ever taught him all this? You must know about him, if, as you say, he was born and bred in your house.

*Men.* And I am certain that no one ever did teach him.

*Soc.* And yet he has the knowledge?

*Men.* The fact, Socrates, is undeniable.

*Soc*. But if he did not acquire the knowledge in this life, then he must have had and learned it at some other time?   86

*Men*. Clearly he must.

*Soc*. Which must have been the time when he was not a man?

*Men*. Yes.

*Soc*. And if there have been always true thoughts in him both at the time when he was and was not a man, which only need to be awakened into knowledge by putting questions to him, his soul must have always possessed this knowledge, for he always either was or was not a man?

*Men*. Obviously.

*Soc*. And if the truth of all things always existed in the soul, then the soul is immortal. Wherefore be of good cheer, and try to recollect what you do not know, or rather what you do not remember.

*Men*. I feel, somehow, that I like what you are saying.

*Soc*. And I, Meno, like what I am saying. Some things I have said of which I am not altogether confident. But that we shall be better and braver and less helpless if we think that we ought to enquire than we should have been if we indulged in the idle fancy that there was no knowing and no use in seeking to know what we do not know;—that is a theme upon which I am ready to fight, in word and deed, to the utmost of my power.

*Men*. There again, Socrates, your words seem to me excellent.

*Soc*. Then, as we are agreed that a man should enquire about that which he does not know, shall you and I make an effort to enquire together into the nature of virtue?

*Men*. By all means, Socrates. And yet I would much rather return to my original question, Whether in seeking to acquire virtue we should regard it as a thing to be taught, or as a gift of nature, or as coming to men in some other way?

*Soc*. Had I the command of you as well as of myself, Meno, I would not have enquired whether virtue is given by instruction or not, until we had first ascertained "what it is." But as you think only of controlling me who am your slave, and never of controlling yourself,—such being your notion of freedom, I must yield to you, for you are irresistible. And therefore I have now to enquire into the qualities of a thing of which I do not as yet know the nature. At any rate, will you condescend a little, and allow the question "Whether virtue is given by instruction, or in any other way," to be argued upon hypothesis? As the geometrician, when he is asked whether a certain  87 triangle is capable of being inscribed in a certain circle,[1] will reply: "I cannot tell you as yet; but I will offer a hypothesis which may assist us in forming a conclusion: If the figure be such that when you have produced a given side of it,[2] the given area of the triangle falls short by an area corresponding to the part produced,[3] then one consequence follows, and if this is impossible then some other; and therefore I wish to assume a hypothesis before I tell you whether this triangle is capable of being inscribed in the circle":—that is a geometrical hypothesis. And we too, as we know not the nature and qualities of virtue, must ask, whether virtue is or is not taught, under a hypothesis: as thus, if virtue is of such a class of mental goods, will it be taught or not? Let the first hypothesis be that virtue is or is not knowledge,—in that case will it be taught or not? or, as we were just now saying, "remembered"? For there is no use in disputing about the name. But is virtue taught or not? or rather, does not every one see that knowledge alone is taught?

*Men.* I agree.

*Soc.* Then if virtue is knowledge, virtue will be taught?

*Men.* Certainly.

*Soc.* Then now we have made a quick end of this question: if virtue is of such a nature, it will be taught; and if not, not?

*Men.* Certainly.

*Soc.* The next question is, whether virtue is knowledge or of another species?

*Men.* Yes, that appears to be the question which comes next in order.

*Soc.* Do we not say that virtue is a good?—This is a hypothesis which is not set aside.

*Men.* Certainly.

*Soc.* Now, if there be any sort of good which is distinct from knowledge, virtue may be that good; but if knowledge embraces all good, then we shall be right in thinking that virtue is knowledge?

*Men.* True.

*Soc.* And virtue makes us good?

*Men.* Yes.

*Soc.* And if we are good, then we are profitable; for all good things are profitable?

[1] Or, whether a certain area is capable of being inscribed as a triangle in a certain circle.

[2] Or, when you apply it to the given line; i.e., the diameter of the circle.

[3] Or, similar to the area so applied.

*Men.* Yes.

*Soc.* Then virtue is profitable?

*Men.* That is the only inference.

*Soc.* Then now let us see what are the things which severally profit us. Health and strength, and beauty and wealth—these, and the like of these, we call profitable?

*Men.* True.

*Soc.* And yet these things may also sometimes do us harm: **88** would you not think so?

*Men.* Yes.

*Soc.* And what is the guiding principle which makes them profitable or the reverse? Are they not profitable when they are rightly used, and hurtful when they are not rightly used?

*Men.* Certainly.

*Soc.* Next, let us consider the goods of the soul: they are temperance, justice, courage, quickness of apprehension, memory, magnanimity, and the like?

*Men.* Surely.

*Soc.* And such of these as are not knowledge, but of another sort, are sometimes profitable and sometimes hurtful; as, for example, courage wanting prudence, which is only a sort of confidence? When a man has no sense he is harmed by courage, but when he has sense he is profited?

*Men.* True.

*Soc.* And the same may be said of temperance and quickness of apprehension; whatever things are learned or done with sense are profitable, but when done without sense they are hurtful?

*Men.* Very true.

*Soc.* And in general, all that the soul attempts or endures, when under the guidance of wisdom, ends in happiness; but when she is under the guidance of folly, in the opposite?

*Men.* That appears to be true.

*Soc.* If then virtue is a quality of the soul, and is admitted to be profitable, it must be wisdom or prudence, since none of the things of the soul are either profitable or hurtful in themselves, but they are all made profitable or hurtful by the addition of wisdom or of folly; and therefore if virtue is profitable, virtue must be a sort of wisdom or prudence?

*Men.* I quite agree.

*Soc.* And the other goods, such as wealth and the like, of which we were just now saying that they are sometimes good and sometimes evil, do not they also become profitable or hurtful, accordingly as the soul guides and uses them rightly or wrongly; just as the things of the soul herself are benefited when under the guidance of wisdom and harmed by folly?

*Men.* True.

*Soc.* And the wise soul guides them rightly, and the foolish soul wrongly.

*Men.* Yes.

*Soc.* And is not this universally true of human nature? All other things hang upon the soul, and the things of the soul herself hang upon 89 wisdom, if they are to be good; and so wisdom is inferred to be that which profits—and virtue, as we say, is profitable?

*Men.* Certainly.

*Soc.* And thus we arrive at the conclusion that virtue is either wholly or partly wisdom?

*Men.* I think that what you are saying, Socrates, is very true.

*Soc.* But if this is true, then the good are not by nature good?

*Men.* I think not.

*Soc.* If they had been, there would assuredly have been discerners of characters among us who would have known our future great men; and on their showing we should have adopted them, and when we had got them, we should have kept them in the citadel out of the way of harm, and set a stamp upon them far rather than upon a piece of gold, in order that no one might tamper with them; and when they grew up they would have been useful to the state?

*Men.* Yes, Socrates, that would have been the right way.

*Soc.* But if the good are not by nature good, are they made good by instruction?

*Men.* There appears to be no other alternative, Socrates. On the supposition that virtue is knowledge, there can be no doubt that virtue is taught.

*Soc.* Yes, indeed; but what if the supposition is erroneous?

*Men.* I certainly thought just now that we were right.

*Soc.* Yes, Meno; but a principle which has any soundness should stand firm not only just now, but always.

*Men.* Well; and why are you so slow of heart to believe that knowledge is virtue?

*Soc.* I will try and tell you why, Meno. I do not retract the assertion that if virtue is knowledge it may be taught; but I fear that I have some reason in doubting whether virtue is knowledge: for consider now and say whether virtue, and not only virtue but anything that is taught, must not have teachers and disciples?

*Men.* Surely.

*Soc.* And conversely, may not the art of which neither teachers nor disciples exist be assumed to be incapable of being taught?

*Men.* True; but do you think that there are no teachers of virtue?

*Soc.* I have certainly often enquired whether there were any, and taken great pains to find them, and have never succeeded; and many have assisted me in the search, and they were the persons whom I thought the most likely to know. Here at the moment when he is wanted we fortunately have sitting by us Anytus, the very person of 90 whom we should make enquiry; to him then let us repair. In the first place, he is the son of a wealthy and wise father, Anthemion, who acquired his wealth, not by accident or gift, like Ismenias the Theban (who has recently made himself as rich as Polycrates), but by his own skill and industry, and who is a well-conditioned, modest man, not insolent, or over-bearing, or annoying; moreover, this son of his has received a good education, as the Athenian people certainly appear to think, for they choose him to fill the highest offices. And these are the sorts of men from whom you are likely to learn whether there are any teachers of virtue, and who they are. Please, Anytus, to help me and your friend Meno in answering our question, Who are the teachers? Consider the matter thus: If we wanted Meno to be a good physician, to whom should we send him? Should we not send him to the physicians?

*Any.* Certainly.

*Soc.* Or if we wanted him to be a good cobbler, should we not send him to the cobblers?

*Any.* Yes.

*Soc.* And so forth?

*Any.* Yes.

*Soc.* Let me trouble you with one more question. When we say that we should be right in sending him to the physicians if we wanted him to be a physician, do we mean that we should be right in sending him to those who profess the art, rather than to those who do not, and to those who demand payment for teaching the art, and profess to teach it to any one who will come and learn? And if these were our reasons, should we not be right in sending him?

*Any.* Yes.

*Soc.* And might not the same be said of flute-playing, and of the other arts? Would a man who wanted to make another a flute-player refuse to send him to those who profess to teach the art for money, and be plaguing other persons to give him instruction, who are not professed teachers and who never had a single disciple in that branch of knowledge which he wishes him to acquire—would not such conduct be the height of folly?

*Any.* Yes, by Zeus, and of ignorance too.

91    *Soc.* Very good. And now you are in a position to advise with me about my friend Meno. He has been telling me, Anytus, that he desires to attain that kind of wisdom and virtue by which men order the state or the house, and honour their parents, and know when to receive and when to send away citizens and strangers, as a good man should. Now, to whom should he go in order that he may learn this virtue? Does not the previous argument imply clearly that we should send him to those who profess and avouch that they are the common teachers of all Hellas, and are ready to impart instruction to any one who likes, at a fixed price?

*Any.* Whom do you mean, Socrates?

*Soc.* You surely know, do you not, Anytus, that these are the people whom mankind call Sophists?

*Any.* By Heracles, Socrates, forbear! I only hope that no friend or kinsman or acquaintance of mine, whether citizen or stranger, will ever be so mad as to allow himself to be corrupted by them; for they are a manifest pest and corrupting influences to those who have to do with them.

*Soc.* What, Anytus? Of all the people who profess that they know how to do men good, do you mean to say that these are the only ones who not only do them no good, but positively corrupt those who are entrusted to them, and in return for this disservice have the face to demand money? Indeed, I cannot believe you; for I know of a single man, Protagoras, who made more out of his craft than the illustrious Pheidias, who created such noble works, or any ten other statuaries. How could that be? A mender of old shoes, or patcher up of clothes, who made the shoes or clothes worse than he received them, could not have remained thirty days undetected, and would very soon have starved; whereas during more than forty years, Protagoras was corrupting all Hellas, and sending his disciples from him worse than he received them, and he was never found out. For, if I am not mistaken, he was about seventy years old at his death, forty of which were spent in the practice of his profession; and during all that time he had a good reputation, which to this day he retains: and not only Protagoras, but many others are well spoken of; some who lived before him, and others who are still living. Now, when you say that they deceived and 92 corrupted the youth, are they to be supposed to have corrupted them consciously or unconsciously? Can those who were deemed by many to be the wisest men of Hellas have been out of their minds?

*Any.* Out of their minds! No, Socrates; the young men who gave their money to them were out of their minds, and their relations and guardians who entrusted their youth to the care of these men were still more out of their minds, and most of all, the cities who allowed them to come in, and did not drive them out, citizen and stranger alike.

*Soc.* Has any of the Sophists wronged you, Anytus? What makes you so angry with them?

*Any.* No, indeed, neither I nor any of my belongings has ever had, nor would I suffer them to have, anything to do with them.

*Soc.* Then you are entirely unacquainted with them?

*Any.* And I have no wish to be acquainted.

*Soc.* Then, my dear friend, how can you know whether a thing is good or bad of which you are wholly ignorant?

*Any.* Quite well; I am sure that I know what manner of men these are, whether I am acquainted with them or not.

*Soc.* You must be a diviner, Anytus, for I really cannot make out, judging from your own words, how, if you are not acquainted with them, you know about them. But I am not enquiring of you who are the teachers who will corrupt Meno (let them be, if you please, the Sophists); I only ask you to tell him who there is in this great city who will teach him how to become eminent in the virtues which I was just now describing. He is the friend of your family, and you will oblige him.

*Any.* Why do you not tell him yourself?

*Soc.* I have told him whom I supposed to be the teachers of these things; but I learn from you that I am utterly at fault, and I dare say that you are right. And now I wish that you, on your part, would tell me to whom among the Athenians he should go. Whom would you name?

*Any.* Why single out individuals? Any Athenian gentleman, taken at random, if he will mind him, will do far more good to him than the Sophists.

*Soc.* And did those gentlemen grow of themselves; and without

93 having been taught by any one, were they nevertheless able to teach others that which they had never learned themselves?

*Any.* I imagine that they learned of the previous generation of gentlemen. Have there not been many good men in this city?

*Soc.* Yes, certainly, Anytus; and many good statesmen also there always have been and there are still, in the city of Athens. But the question is whether they were also good teachers of their own virtue;—not whether there are, or have been, good men in this part of the world, but whether virtue can be taught is the question which we have been discussing. Now, do we mean to say that the good men of our own and of other times knew how to impart to others that virtue which they had themselves; or is virtue a thing incapable of being communicated or imparted by one man to another? That is the question which I and Meno have been arguing. Look at the matter in your own way: Would you not admit that Themistocles was a good man?

*Any.* Certainly; no man better.

*Soc.* And must not he then have been a good teacher, if any man ever was a good teacher, of his own virtue?

*Any.* Yes, certainly,—if he wanted to be so.

*Soc.* But would he not have wanted? He would, at any rate, have desired to make his own son a good man and a gentleman; he could not have been jealous of him, or have intentionally abstained from imparting to him his own virtue. Did you never hear that he made his son Cleophantus a famous horseman; and had him taught to stand upright on horseback and hurl a javelin, and to do many other marvellous things; and in anything which could be learned from a master he was well trained? Have you not heard from our elders of him?

*Any.* I have.

*Soc.* Then no one could say that his son showed any want of capacity?

*Any.* Very likely not.

*Soc.* But did any one, old or young, ever say in our hearing that Cleophantus, son of Themistocles, was a wise or good man, as his father was?

*Any.* I have certainly never heard any one say so.

*Soc.* And if virtue could have been taught, would his father Themistocles have sought to train him in these minor accomplishments, and allowed him who, as you must remember, was his own son, to be no better than his neighbours in those qualities in which he himself excelled?

*Any.* Indeed, indeed, I think not.

*Soc.* Here was a teacher of virtue whom you admit to be among the best men of the past. Let us take another,—Aristides, the son of 94 Lysimachus: would you not acknowledge that he was a good man?

*Any.* To be sure I should.

*Soc.* And did not he train his son Lysimachus better than any other Athenian in all that could be done for him by the help of masters? But what has been the result? Is he a bit better than any other mortal? He is an acquaintance of yours, and you see what he is like. There is Pericles, again, magnificent in his wisdom; and he, as you are aware, had two sons, Paralus and Xanthippus.

*Any.* I know.

*Soc.* And you know, also, that he taught them to be unrivalled horsemen, and had them trained in music and gymnastics and all sorts of arts—in these respects they were on a level with the best—and had he no wish to make good men of them? Nay, he must have wished it. But virtue, as I suspect, could not be taught. And that you may not suppose the incompetent teachers to be only the meaner sort of Athenians and few in number, remember again that Thucydides had two sons, Melesias and Stephanus, whom, besides giving them a good education in other things, he trained in wrestling, and they were the best wrestlers in Athens: one of them he committed to the care of Xanthias, and the other of Eudorus, who had the reputation of being the most celebrated wrestlers of that day. Do you remember them?

*Any.* I have heard of them.

*Soc.* Now, can there be a doubt that Thucydides, whose children were taught things for which he had to spend money, would have taught them to be good men, which would have cost him nothing, if virtue could have been taught? Will you reply that he was a mean man, and had not many friends among the Athenians and allies? Nay, but he was of a great family, and a man of influence at Athens and in all Hellas, and, if virtue could have been taught, he would have found out some Athenian or foreigner who would have made good men of his sons, if he could not himself spare the time from cares of state. Once more, I suspect, friend Anytus, that virtue is not a thing which can be taught?

*Any.* Socrates, I think that you are too ready to speak evil of men: and, if you will take my advice, I would recommend you to be careful. Perhaps there is no city in which it is not easier to do men harm than to do them good, and this is certainly the case at Athens, as 95 I believe that you know.

*Soc.* O Meno, I think that Anytus is in a rage. And he may well be in a rage, for he thinks, in the first place, that I am defaming these gentlemen; and in the second place, he is of opinion that he is one of them himself. But some day he will know what is the meaning of defamation, and if he ever does, he will forgive me. Meanwhile I will return to you, Meno; for I suppose that there are gentlemen in your region too?

*Men.* Certainly there are.

*Soc.* And are they willing to teach the young? and do they profess to be teachers? and do they agree that virtue is taught?

*Men.* No indeed, Socrates, they are anything but agreed; you may hear them saying at one time that virtue can be taught, and then again the reverse.

*Soc.* Can we call those teachers who do not acknowledge the possibility of their own vocation?

*Men.* I think not, Socrates.

*Soc.* And what do you think of these Sophists, who are the only professors? Do they seem to you to be teachers of virtue?

*Men.* I often wonder, Socrates, that Gorgias is never heard promising to teach virtue: and when he hears others promising he only laughs at them; but he thinks that men should be taught to speak.

*Soc.* Then do you not think that the Sophists are teachers?

*Men.* I cannot tell you, Socrates; like the rest of the world, I am in doubt, and sometimes I think that they are teachers and sometimes not.

*Soc.* And are you aware that not you only and other politicians have doubts whether virtue can be taught or not, but that Theognis the poet says the very same thing?

*Men.* Where does he say so?

*Soc.* In these elegiac verses:

Eat and drink and sit with the mighty, and make yourself agreeable to them; for from the good you will learn what is good, but if you mix with the bad you will lose the intelligence which you already have.

Do you observe that here he seems to imply that virtue can be taught?

*Men.* Clearly.

*Soc.* But in some other verses he shifts about and says:

If understanding could be created and put into a man, then they [who were able to perform this feat] would have obtained great rewards.

And again:

> Never would a bad son have sprung from a good sire, for he would have heard the voice of instruction; but not by teaching will you ever make 96 a bad man into a good one.

And this, as you may remark, is a contradiction of the other.

*Men.* Clearly.

*Soc.* And is there anything else of which the professors are affirmed not only not to be teachers of others, but to be ignorant themselves, and bad at the knowledge of that which they are professing to teach? or is there anything about which even the acknowledged "gentlemen" are sometimes saying that "this thing can be taught," and sometimes the opposite? Can you say that they are teachers in any true sense whose ideas are in such confusion?

*Men.* I should say, certainly not.

*Soc.* But if neither the Sophists nor the gentlemen are teachers, clearly there can be no other teachers?

*Men.* No.

*Soc.* And if there are no teachers, neither are there disciples?

*Men.* Agreed.

*Soc.* And we have admitted that a thing cannot be taught of which there are neither teachers nor disciples?

*Men.* We have.

*Soc.* And there are no teachers of virtue to be found anywhere?

*Men.* There are not.

*Soc.* And if there are no teachers, neither are there scholars?

*Men.* That, I think, is true.

*Soc.* Then virtue cannot be taught?

*Men.* Not if we are right in our view. But I cannot believe, Socrates, that there are no good men: And if there are, how did they come into existence?

*Soc.* I am afraid, Meno, that you and I are not good for much, and that Gorgias has been as poor an educator of you as Prodicus has been of me. Certainly we shall have to look to ourselves, and try to find some one who will help in some way or other to improve us. This I say, because I observe that in the previous discussion none of us remarked that right and good action is possible to man under other guidance than that of knowledge (ἐπιστήμη)—and indeed if this be denied, there is no seeing how there can be any good men at all.

*Men.* How do you mean, Socrates?

*Soc.* I mean that good men are necessarily useful or profitable.
97 Were we not right in admitting this? It must be so.

*Men.* Yes.

*Soc.* And in supposing that they will be useful only if they are
true guides to us of action—there we were also right?

*Men.* Yes.

*Soc.* But when we said that a man cannot be a good guide unless
he have knowledge (φϱόνησις), in this we were wrong.

*Men.* What do you mean by the word "right"?

*Soc.* I will explain. If a man knew the way to Larisa, or anywhere else, and went to the place and led others thither, would he not
be a right and good guide?

*Men.* Certainly.

*Soc.* And a person who had a right opinion about the way, but
had never been and did not know, might be a good guide also, might
he not?

*Men.* Certainly.

*Soc.* And while he has true opinion about that which the other
knows, he will be just as good a guide if he thinks the truth, as he who
knows the truth?

*Men.* Exactly.

*Soc.* Then true opinion is as good a guide to correct action as
knowledge; and that was the point which we omitted in our specula-
tion about the nature of virtue, when we said that knowledge only is
the guide of right action; whereas there is also right opinion.

*Men.* True.

*Soc.* Then right opinion is not less useful than knowledge?

*Men.* The difference, Socrates, is only that he who has knowledge will always be right; but he who has right opinion will sometimes
be right, and sometimes not.

*Soc.* What do you mean? Can he be wrong who has right opinion, so long as he has right opinion?

*Men.* I admit the cogency of your argument, and therefore, Socrates, I wonder that knowledge should be preferred to right opinion—
or why they should ever differ.

*Soc.* And shall I explain this wonder to you?

*Men.* Do tell me.

*Soc.* You would not wonder if you had ever observed the images
of Daedalus; but perhaps you have not got them in your country?

*Men.* What have they to do with the question?

*Soc.* Because they require to be fastened in order to keep them, and if they are not fastened they will play truant and run away.

*Men.* Well, what of that?

*Soc.* I mean to say that they are not very valuable possessions if they are at liberty, for they will walk off like runaway slaves; but when fastened, they are of great value, for they are really beautiful works of art. Now this is an illustration of the nature of true opinions: while they abide with us they are beautiful and fruitful, but they run away out of the human soul, and do not remain long, and therefore they are not of much value until they are fastened by the tie of the cause; and this fastening of them, friend Meno, is recollection, as you and I have agreed to call it. But when they are bound, in the first place, they have the nature of knowledge; and, in the second place, they are abiding. And this is why knowledge is more honourable and excellent than true opinion, because fastened by a chain.

*Men.* What you are saying, Socrates, seems to be very like the truth.

*Soc.* I too speak rather in ignorance; I only conjecture. And yet that knowledge differs from true opinion is no matter of conjecture with me. There are not many things which I profess to know, but this is most certainly one of them.

*Men.* Yes, Socrates; and you are quite right in saying so.

*Soc.* And am I not also right in saying that true opinion leading the way perfects action quite as well as knowledge?

*Men.* There again, Socrates, I think you are right.

*Soc.* Then right opinion is not a whit inferior to knowledge, or less useful in action; nor is the man who has right opinion inferior to him who has knowledge?

*Men.* True.

*Soc.* And surely the good man has been acknowledged by us to be useful?

*Men.* Yes.

*Soc.* Seeing then that men become good and useful to states, not only because they have knowledge, but because they have right opinion, and that neither knowledge nor right opinion is given to man by nature or acquired by him—(do you imagine either of them to be given by nature?

*Men.* Not I.)

*Soc.* Then if they are not given by nature, neither are the good by nature good?

*Men.* Certainly not.

*Soc.* And nature being excluded, then came the question whether virtue is acquired by teaching?

*Men.* Yes.

*Soc.* If virtue was wisdom [or knowledge], then, as we thought, it was taught?

*Men.* Yes.

*Soc.* And if it was taught it was wisdom?

*Men.* Certainly.

*Soc.* And if there were teachers, it might be taught; and if there were no teachers, not?

*Men.* True.

*Soc.* But surely we acknowledged that there were no teachers of virtue?

*Men.* Yes.

*Soc.* Then we acknowledged that it was not taught, and was not wisdom?

*Men.* Certainly.

*Soc.* And yet we admitted that it was a good?

*Men.* Yes.

99     *Soc.* And the right guide is useful and good?

*Men.* Certainly.

*Soc.* And the only right guides are knowledge and true opinion—these are the guides of man; for things which happen by chance are not under the guidance of man: but the guides of man are true opinion and knowledge.

*Men.* I think so too.

*Soc.* But if virtue is not taught, neither is virtue knowledge.

*Men.* Clearly not.

*Soc.* Then of two good and useful things, one, which is knowledge, has been set aside, and cannot be supposed to be our guide in political life.

*Men.* I think not.

*Soc.* And therefore not by any wisdom, and not because they were wise, did Themistocles and those others of whom Anytus spoke govern states. This was the reason why they were unable to make others like themselves—because their virtue was not grounded on knowledge.

*Men.* That is probably true, Socrates.

*Soc.* But if not by knowledge, the only alternative which remains is that statesmen must have guided states by right opinion, which is in politics what divination is in religion; for diviners and also prophets say many things truly, but they know not what they say.

*Men.* So I believe.

*Soc.* And may we not, Meno, truly call those men "divine" who, having no understanding, yet succeed in many a grand deed and word?

*Men.* Certainly.

*Soc.* Then we shall also be right in calling divine those whom we were just now speaking of as diviners and prophets, including the whole tribe of poets. Yes, and statesmen above all may be said to be divine and illumined, being inspired and possessed of God, in which condition they say many grand things, not knowing what they say.

*Men.* Yes.

*Soc.* And the women too, Meno, call good men divine—do they not? and the Spartans, when they praise a good man, say "that he is a divine man."

*Men.* And I think, Socrates, that they are right; although very likely our friend Anytus may take offence at the word.

*Soc.* I do not care; as for Anytus, there will be another opportunity of talking with him. To sum up our enquiry—the result seems to be, if we are at all right in our view, that virtue is neither natural nor acquired, but an instinct given by God to the virtuous. Nor is the 100 instinct accompanied by reason, unless there may be supposed to be among statesmen some one who is capable of educating statesmen. And if there be such an one, he may be said to be among the living what Homer says that Tiresias was among the dead, "he alone has understanding; but the rest are flitting shades"; and he and his virtue in like manner will be a reality among shadows.

*Men.* That is excellent, Socrates.

*Soc.* Then, Meno, the conclusion is that virtue comes to the virtuous by the gift of God. But we shall never know the certain truth until, before asking how virtue is given, we enquire into the actual nature of virtue. I fear that I must go away, but do you, now that you are persuaded yourself, persuade our friend Anytus. And do not let him be so exasperated; if you can conciliate him, you will have done good service to the Athenian people.

# EDUCATION*

## *F. J. E. Woodbridge*

Can virtue, then, be taught? Can education make a man good? The question is asked again and again in Plato's pages, but never receives a straightforward, unequivocal answer. It is left a question, the insistent human question as we make our way through the changes and chances of this mortal life. Meno puts it squarely in his conversation with Socrates: "Can you tell me, Socrates, if virtue is teachable? If not teachable, is it a matter of discipline? If neither a matter of discipline nor learned, is it acquired by men as they grow, or in some other way?" Socrates confesses at once that he knows nothing whatever about the matter and has never met a man that does. He is willing, however, to talk about it with Meno. They talk, and the result is a demonstration of their confusion. They are as ignorant at the end as they were in the beginning. They cannot tell what virtue is and cannot, therefore, answer the questions asked. They admit, however, that, whatever it is, it is adventitious. It comes to men. It does not, as yet, come by teaching, for although there are professed teachers of it, neither parents nor professors succeed. It does not come by discipline, for the same discipline produces contrary results. It does not come to men as they grow, for some grow virtuous and others vicious. How, then, does it come? Let us say by divine favor. It is a gift which the gods occasionally bestow. For do not all men praise virtue, exact it, call it divine, look upon it as something rare and exceptional, something alien to our nature, but akin to divinity? "Even the women, Meno, call good men divine, and the Spartans, when they praise a good man, say, 'This man is divine.'" Virtue comes, but it comes by grace. We must wait for it.

It is instructive to wait with Meno and Socrates. The former wants his question answered, but the latter keeps insisting that we must first seek out what virtue is. Meno gets tired of the search. He

* From *The Son of Apollo* by F. J. E. Woodbridge (Boston: Houghton Mifflin, 1929), pp. 127–147. Reprinted by permission of Houghton Mifflin Company.

recalls a current argument that it is useless to search for what you know and equally useless to search for that of which you are wholly ignorant. Socrates appeals to the soul. It is undying, but born many times and has in these changes seen and known all things in heaven and earth, but its knowledge is obscured or forgotten and needs to be recalled to mind. For learning is only remembering. Our searchings are the proddings of our memories. We should take heart, therefore, and continue. Meno is unconvinced and asks for proof. His slave is standing near, knowing how to speak Greek, but knowing nothing about geometry. Socrates questions the boy and begs Meno to observe carefully whether the boy is learning from Socrates or only remembering. And the unlearned slave discovers the solution of the problem of doubling the square. It was an impressive performance, one which has caught the imagination of many readers and been taken neatly to illustrate Plato's doctrine of knowledge. "Our birth is but a sleep and a forgetting." Yet a reader may well ask why a problem in geometry was solved instead of the quest for virtue ended. The situation demanded that virtue be found. Why did Socrates not dig it out of the boy's soul instead of a square twice as big as another? The problem in geometry had been solved again and again. Both Socrates and Meno knew the solution. But they did not know what virtue is. They had prodded their own memories in vain. What a demonstration it would have been to reveal it by prodding the memory of a slave! Others than Plato have done it.

The demonstration seems to have astonished Meno a little, but not to have wholly convinced him. Socrates would resume the quest for virtue, but Meno declined. Apparently the solution of geometrical problems was of no help. He returns to his original question. Can virtue be taught? Socrates consents to attack it, abandoning the greater quest, but would proceed hypothetically as geometricians do when they are not very sure of what they are talking about. Let us suppose that virtue belongs to the class of teachable things. Then, if it is teachable, it must be knowledge, for what is teachable is always knowledge. But if it is knowledge and, therefore, teachable, there should be teachers of it. But there are no teachers of it. Therefore, it is not knowledge and is not teachable. The argument is not impressive, but the illustrations of it are. Socrates appeals to human experience, to the widespread interest in education, to the efforts parents make in behalf of their children, to the money they spend, paying it even to gross imposters—and all without effect. There are the sons of Pericles, for example. Could sons be more favorably situated for getting the best that life can give? But look at them! They were both found in the company with Protagoras when Socrates took Hippocrates to be introduced to that great master. You can teach Meno's slave geometry, but you cannot teach the sons of Pericles virtue. Socrates does not say that in words, but the "Meno" says it in effect and says it more clearly than it says anything else. Geometry can be taught under the most unfavorable conditions, but virtue cannot be taught under the most favorable. That is Platonic doctrine. We see the boys of Lysimachus and Melesias waiting while their parents, two generals, and Socrates get educated; we see Hippocrates rushing off at dawn to Protagoras to be forgotten; we see the sons of Pericles, corrupted in spite of every advantage; and we see Meno's slave solving a geometrical problem in five minutes. Would Plato have us believe that this is what education is?

We read the "Laches," the "Protagoras," the "Meno," and other comments of Plato on education and may ask what we have learned. Perhaps, however, the question is ill-advised. Perhaps Plato expects the reader not to learn, but to see, or to learn only after he has seen. What is education and what is virtue? The fact is that everybody seems to know. There seems to be no need of a demonstration to show that every life, that of man, woman, or child, of ruler or ruled, of statesman or flute-player, of doctor or carpenter, of free man or slave, should have a quality which commends it irrespective of all distinctions of age, sex, and occupation. That quality is virtue, a certain harmony of character which guarantees the finding, in its possessor, of a man indeed. The quality may be conceived nobly or ignobly, sanely or sentimentally, conventionally or unconventionally. The great matter is its possession—even among thieves with their honor. It is the one thing without which no life, no matter how fortunate and successful it may be in other respects, can be wholly satisfactory and with which almost any life is lifted high. It gives the supreme distinction to a man, enhancing all his natural or acquired gifts and powers. It makes of him a personality, a soul as distinct from a body, and lets him live mindful of the things that do not perish in spite of the many births and deaths of human bodies. So all men really want it. down in the bottom of their hearts. They want it for themselves: they expect it of others. And most of all, they want it for their children. New lives, as yet unsoiled by what the old remember, suggest possibilities and splendors. Symbols of hope, they give promise of the better day. They are the future, bidding the dead past bury its dead. Yes; everybody knows what virtue is—knows that it is the force which transforms a body into a soul. Like Laches we may not be able to define it nicely, but we think we can tell it when we see it. And our saddest moments are those when we have relied on its presence, but found it was far away.

That is one of the things which Plato would have his readers see. He is a realist through and through. Socrates seeks and seeks. He does not find what he seeks. But he finds other seekers—the ambitious, the misguided, the deluded, the visionary, the mercenary, the weak, the confident, the boastful. He alone is disillusioned. In the light of that disillusionment the others are seen to be what they are, seekers of something which, if they have it, they do not have because they have sought it. They have it by divine favor. On that same disillusionment, Socrates builds the doctrine that no man willingly does wrong. It has the look of a strange doctrine which human experience hardly seems to justify. Some men appear to glory in evil which they willingly and knowingly do. Others claim that they are carried about against their wills by passions, temptations, and allurements; they are beside themselves when they sin. To all this Socrates replies: evil is, admittedly, an injury to the soul and no man willingly injures his soul. The reply may not produce conviction, but Socrates found it difficult to win from those he questioned the admission that they themselves were really guilty of that injury. Some were ready enough to admit that their souls had been hurt by their own deeds and those of others. They were not ready to admit, however, that their own deeds were done with that intent, although the deeds of others may have been malicious. Driven to face that admission squarely, they refused, confessing the moral egotism that lies in the breast of every child of Adam. This is what the doctrine of Socrates exposes. The egotism is not condemned. It is exposed as a fact. It is made to illuminate human conduct. It reveals men working for their own good no matter how strange that working may look at times. Moral egotism may make a man believe that he knows what is best for himself and for others also. He is fortunate and divinely favored if he does, and, acting on that knowledge, becomes a benefactor of his kind. It may humble him to confess that such knowledge is not his and yet fortify him in the conviction that he does the best he can under the circumstances. Whatever effects similar to these it may have on individuals, it has one common effect—it generates the need of knowledge. For man lives in a precarious world. He must take thought to live well. He does not willingly do wrong, so, if he does wrong as he so often does, the reason lies in his ignorance. He has not had full command of the situation. He has not been far-sighted enough or he has not had time to take into consideration all that should be taken into consideration. He wanted to act or had to act. He might have prepared himself better or been better prepared by others. A man may make a pair of shoes badly or play the flute badly without either wanting or being willing to do so. He can be taught to do both better. May he not be taught also to live better? If his moral egotism prevents him from doing wrong willingly and convinces him that he does the best he can under the circumstances, would not the proper education help him? Surely there must be those to whom he might go for advice and direction, some one who knows the soul, a psychologist, if you will. Not ourselves, but our education is responsible for what we are. Let us reform it. But you can teach Meno's slave geometry; you cannot teach the sons of Pericles virtue. Moral egotism begets the faith in education. Everybody believes in it—Catholics and Protestants, individualists and socialists, capitalists and communists, despots and anarchists, conservatives and radicals. And we all look for the new school while Meno's slave and the sons of Pericles look on.

This also Plato would have his readers see before they ask what they have learned. Is there anything to learn from the spectacle? Or is the son of Apollo letting the god in him smile at the man in him, inviting our divinity to smile with him at our humanity? It is difficult to decide with confidence. Yet it is clear that the "Laches," the "Protagoras," and the "Meno" are, first of all, dramatic scenes. If they are regarded as contributions to the theory or practice of education or to a theory of ethics, they do not themselves disclose what that contribution is. The reader is left precisely in the same predicament as the characters in the dialogues are left. Nothing is settled either for him or for them. The things they both want settled are postponed and cannot be settled until something else is done which they have not been able to do. This something has never yet been done and the dialogues give no assurance that it ever will be done. Their inconclusiveness is evidently deliberate and intended. Yet the reader gets an impression of something quite different from futility. He has been shown that virtue cannot be defined and that faith in education is vain, but it is not likely that he will accept either demonstration. He is very far from being convinced. Like Socrates, he is inclined to think that on another occasion, under better circumstances, with more knowledge and study, he could do much better. He is a little amused and a little impatient at waiting for divine favor. Grace may have a charming sound, but it is hollow as the final word in the solution of social problems. Why not, then, take this natural effect on the reader as the intended effect of the dialogues? They are not treatises on education. They are the dramatic rendering of a human interest and a human faith. They present, in spite of their local limitations, faithful pictures of the situation in which we still find ourselves. A Socrates may rarely go about among us, but when he does, we see the man fighting in armor, the new school, Lysimachus, Melesias, with their boys, Laches, Nisias, Hippocrates, Protagoras, Meno, the slave, and the sons of Pericles. There is the expectation of grace. Our men in armor and our Protagorases need not be named. Would Socrates find them enjoying, in addition to the applause and fees of men, the favor of the gods? And if he did not, would the moneys spent on education be much diminished or interest in it flag? It is the drama of education that is found in Plato.

The drama may be as instructive as a treatise. Why has not virtue been long ago defined? Why has not education long ago removed our social ills? It is easy to answer that we do not know sufficiently the nature of the human soul, that the psychologists have not been given enough control, or that God's grace has not descended amply enough. It is either our temporary ignorance or our natural depravity which is to blame. Let it be so. But the drama makes it sun-clear that there is something at once comic and tragic in the expectation that we can find teachers who are neither ignorant nor naturally depraved. Parents are notoriously bad educators of their children and the sons of psychologists seem to be no better off than the sons of Pericles. Parents, therefore, should not be educators, at least they should not be educators of their own children. Send the children to school! Let them be educated by the childless or by the parents of other children! Get them out of the home and into an institution! Humble the family and exalt the state! This is precisely what Plato recommends in the "Republic." And this is precisely what we keep on recommending. But the school asks for children better trained at home and the home asks for children better trained at school. Hippocrates, that boy of the new day, is either forgotten or experimented upon while parents and teachers' associations debate. They discover that it is parents, and not children that need education. Perhaps it is the children who do the educating after all. If only we, who were once children, could understand them! The hope of education lies in understanding the child and in training him accordingly.

It may be that none will find instruction in Plato's ironical exhibition of the mixture of comedy and tragedy in the human drama of education. Yet it seems clear that Plato, and Greek philosophy generally, thought that there was something salutary simply in seeing things as they are. The spectacle of life fascinates. Caught in the turmoil of affairs, we do not see it clearly, for our eyes are fixed on other things, our business, our wealth, our occupations, our reputation. These give us a bias and a preoccupation which prevents our seeing the spectacle we make of ourselves. But in moments of leisure we flock to the theater or read stories of love, passion, intrigue, and adventure. These, and not our experience, tell us what life really is, for they transform us from participants in action to spectators of it. This justifies our presence in the theater. Surrounded by strangers and intimates we do not blush to look at scenes in which we would never willingly be found in action, or hear words we would never willingly be overheard using. We have the happiness of detachment. We may laugh or cry without having anything whatever at stake and without the moral obligation to interfere with what is going on. We see life without living it. Like disembodied souls we enjoy the essences of joy and sorrow, love and hate, life and death, laughter and tears, without the consequences they have in a society of bodies. Art, not business or work or morals or religion or science or philanthropy, reveals what life is and reveals it to be viewed in freedom. By it we escape from living. From it we may get pleasure and illumination. If we get the former only, the trouble is either with the art or with ourselves. If we get the latter, then we know better what we are doing when we meddle to make men better. So, if we asked Plato to tell us the reason why education has not been more successful, he might only give us another dialogue, but he might also, as man to man, say that it was neither our ignorance nor our depravity, but rather our failure to see what education is. With that vision we may not educate the better, but we shall at least know what we are doing.

If we cannot teach virtue, we may teach geometry. Inability to do the one is no excuse for not doing the other or for doing it badly. Plato seems to have been fond of geometry and to have recommended it highly. There is an incredible but illustrative story that he made it an entrance requirement to the Academy. The story is true of colleges of today. In spite of the fact that knowing that the square on the diagonal is twice the square on the side does not improve a child's manners or morals, our schools generally, and some parents, have persisted in the belief that a child who cannot master that piece of knowledge has not the best of prospects for the future. He is looked upon with some suspicion and is a cause of some anxiety. Capacity for virtue in him is not as well-assured as one could wish. His inability seems to imply a defect somewhere in his soul. He has failed in a test of intelligence. He may be a good child and turn out to be a good man in spite of it, but it is a little remarkable that he should. There are vast realms of knowledge from which he is excluded and these realms happen to be of considerable importance for the business, comforts, and conveniences of life. The intellectually defective may, none the less, get through life with a fair or even a remarkable showing, but there is always the danger of intellectual and moral crookedness in them. Thoughtless people may not be bad. It is something of a miracle, however, if they are good, a miracle of grace which has blest them with a lovable nature or a generous disposition. It may be no less a miracle when the thoughtful are good. Geometry is not a guarantee of virtue. There are many mathematicians who are not virtuous, who are notoriously queer and unsociable, and who have the wildest fancies. Yet society keeps on putting its faith in men who do not double squares by doubling their sides. So much in life depends on finding diagonals, that the highest rewards await the men who can find them. So we stick to teaching geometry. Slaves look less like slaves when they can master it and the sons of Pericles are certainly not doing mischief when they study it.

Geometry is not the only thing that can be taught nor the only thing that Plato recommends. It is, however, the study which in many ways best illustrates his recommendations—those recommendations which his dramatizing of education seems to disclose. For geometry is the high road to the certain and the inevitable. It forbids differences of opinion. It may let a man start as he likes and give him, like the souls in Er's story, a free choice to begin with, but after that he is in the hands of fate, compelled possibly to eat his own children. Like Thomas Hobbes, studying geometry at the age of forty, he may exclaim, "By God! it's impossible," only to yield to conviction in the end. Plato seems to think that experiences of that sort are good for both man and child. He would not have teachers ask: What is *your* opinion? What do *you* think? How does it impress *you?* How does it *seem* to *you?* Socrates, indeed goes about asking just such questions, but he asks them to expose ignorance, not to discover knowledge, and he claims again and again that he is no teacher. He was charged with corrupting the young and put to death as a consequence. History, shocked at the injustice of it, has pronounced him blameless and accounted him one of the greatest benefactors of mankind. It is clear, however, that Plato does not recommend the Socratic method for any other purpose than that for which Socrates used it. He exposes our ignorance that we may flee to geometry and studies like it. When Socrates does teach, he leaves the sons of Pericles with Protagoras and talks to Meno's slave about a square. He is everlastingly trying to get men, old and young, out of the realm of *their* opinions and into the realm of fixed and certain knowledge. His abomination is the doctrine that everything flows, nothing abides. Men must be made conscious, even if he must drink hemlock, that *their* opinions may be of very little consequence in a world in which they are born without their consent and out of which they go against their will. They are in God's hands, not their own, and their one hope of salvation lies in finding out how God's hands work, not in boasting of the work of their own. In spite of poets, who so often do him grave injustice, God is not an opinionated person who at one time thinks he knows and at another changes his mind. He is rather like geometry which lets you start as you will and overtakes you in the end. Play the flute and debate with Protagoras; get angry with him even and change your mind and his about virtue; but be sure all the time that you can tell what is the double of a square. Perhaps the forgotten Hippocrates learned something after all and went home to study geometry. Did he thereby become a slave or put himself in the way of God's grace?

The distinction between debatable and undebatable subjects—between opinion and knowledge—abounds in the dialogues of Plato. It is epitomized in the distinction between virtue and geometry. Virtue cannot be taught because it is debatable, while geometry can, just because it is not debatable. From the contrast emerges a principle: the teachability of subjects varies with their debatable character. And the principle furnishes some guidance for the ordering of a young man's studies. He should proceed from the undebatable to the debatable, from the realm of knowledge to the realm of opinion. He should not proceed conversely. This latter way may, doubtless, be more exciting, more stimulating, and more spectacular, for the young alone are precocious and can be pushed with little effort to express with confidence opinions which astonish their elders. Their parents, anxious about their education and hopeful for their future, are readily impressed by any evidence of precociousness and would gladly see in it proof of the presence of genius. There is, besides, something eloquent and arresting in the spectacle of a young man of twenty having settled so soon questions which his parents, at the end of their lives, find have never been settled to their own satisfaction. Yet the admiration dims a little when youth begins to instruct age, finds fault with its convictions and prejudices, demands to take the realm of opinion in its own hands, and justifies the demand by what has gone on in the school. Nature, thinks Plato, has provided enough healthy opposition between youth and age to make us cautious of increasing it by education. He seriously questions whether the young have any right to opinions about the unsettled before they have reasonably mastered the settled. His reason is profound. It is not that he would keep things forever as they are, for he put the perfect city in the sky where it need never change and let Ulysses make the choice we are to remember. He was a revolutionist, a man of novel ideas, and Socrates was put to death. Clearly his recommendation is not that of the stand-patter. His reason is that disinterested discipline may give a man balance, while interested discipline most assuredly will not. He knew well enough that opinions early formed are the hardest to outgrow, and when outgrown often leave a man without chart or compass, while those later formed are far more susceptible to change and adjustment. In spite of the protests of youth, it is age and experience which are liberal. It is age and experience that hesitate to cramp and confine and to close the door of opportunity, for, otherwise, youth would not be allowed to be what it is. It is not young men who do justice, but old men, even rich old men like Cephalus, who do it and do it without troubling themselves very much about what it is. So Plato would keep the young out of the realm of the debatable until they had matured a little in the realm of the undebatable. Then he would let them into the former, trusting the grace of God to do the rest.

It is, thus, disinterested schooling which Plato puts first, the study of those subjects in which personal opinions do not count. He would have children play and dance and sing and even go to church, for such exercises he thought cultivate their bodies, their sociability, and their sense of reverence. But he would have them taught very little about God or virtue. He would not let them think that such matters were in their province to decide, but he would cultivate in them the habit of making decisions. That was one reason why he found geometry useful. Meno's slave thought at first that the doubled square would have a side double that of the original, but was led to discover his mistake and discover it beyond the shadow of a doubt. He found that his opinion was rectified by finding that his opinion did not count. Simply by following the lead of the square itself he came to the right decision and that decision held whether he were slave or free, young or old, virtuous or vicious. It was a disinterested decision, the kind of decision which the young should be encouraged to make as a preparation for making decisions which are not disinterested. They may think, or they may be told by some sophist, that solving problems in mathematics or in science, in language, in history, or in economics, which have long since been solved over and over again and which involve no living issues of the current world, is a bore, a waste of time, and a poor preparation for life. Plato, however, advises us to keep on. He believes that such a discipline is the best possible anticipation of the hard knocks which experience will surely bring later. For as the habit of being led by what one studies to disinterested decisions grows, the soul grows more and more immune to vanity, to self-deception, and to despair. It becomes catholic, liberal, and generous. A soul may not be taught virtue, but it may be prepared for it through habits of disinterestedness.

# THE SOCRATIC PARADOXES*

## Gerasimos Santas

Plato's ethics in the earlier dialogues (at least up to the *Republic*) is characterized by two doctrines commonly known as the Socratic paradoxes. The first of these is that no one desires evil things and that all who pursue evil things do so involuntarily;[1] the second doctrine is that virtue is knowledge and that all who do injustice or wrong do so involuntarily.[2]

Students of Plato have found these doctrines puzzling and paradoxical. It is not difficult to see why. We commonly think that men sometimes harm themselves knowing that they are doing so, and that often they do what is morally wrong knowing that it is morally wrong when it is in their power to do otherwise. Incontinence and moral weakness are supposed to be familiar facts of experience; yet the doctrines just mentioned seem to contradict these facts. How are we to account for this? Are we to suppose that Plato held, and held most persistently through several dialogues, views that contradict facts with which presumably everyone is acquainted?

Most students of Plato have supposed just this. T. Gomperz, for example, writes:

Such a thing as knowing what is right and yet disobeying that knowledge, believing an action wrong and yet yielding to the motives that impel to it, is for Socrates not merely a sad and disastrous occurrence; it is a sheer impossibility. He does not combat or condemn, he simply denies, that state of mind which his contemporaries called "being overcome by desire." . . .

* From *The Philosophical Review*, LXXIII (1964), 147–164. Reprinted by permission of the author and *The Philosophical Review*.

1 *Meno* 77b–78b, *Prot.* 358c, *Gorg.* 468c5–7. Numbers and letters refer to the Stephanus pages and page sections, except for the numbers that follow the letters, which refer to the lines in the edition of John Burnet, *Platonis Opera* (Oxford, 1903–1907). The translations are those of the Loeb Classical Library unless otherwise indicated.

2 *Gorg.* 460b–d, 509e5–7; *Prot.* 345e, 360d3; indirect statements of the doctrine occur in *Meno* 87, 89; *Laches* 198; *Charm.* 173.

Although the state of mind whose existence is denied by Socrates does really occur, its occurrence is a far rarer phenomenon than is generally supposed.[3]

This opinion, that the Socratic paradoxes contradict facts, is shared by Aristotle, St. Thomas Aquinas, W. Jaeger, F. M. Cornford, and others;[4] indeed it is no exaggeration to say that it is the received opinion about the paradoxes.[5]

An idea behind this widespread interpretation is that Plato over-emphasized the intellect and neglected—even entirely neglected—the will (this tendency in Plato's thought is usually labeled "intellectualism").[6] Perhaps the best general statement of this idea has been made by John Gould, who, in interpreting Aristotle's criticism, says:

Socrates was wrong in supposing that if a man achieved an understanding of what justice involves, he would necessarily become just in behavior, since the whole problem of choice intervenes between knowledge and action.[7]

I think that this interpretation of the Socratic paradoxes is at the very least partly mistaken, though not at all for the reasons that Gould gives.[8] It is the aim of this paper to show that Plato does not deny the fact of moral weakness and that his views concerning the relation of knowledge to conduct are far more plausible than they are usually supposed to be. I shall begin by drawing a distinction between the two doctrines stated in the beginning, calling the first a "prudential paradox" and the second a "moral paradox"; I shall then consider each of these in turn.

[3] *Greek Thinkers,* trans. by G. G. Berry (London, 1905), II, 67.

[4] *Nic. Ethics* 1145b22–29; St. Thomas Aquinas, *Philosophical Texts,* trans. and ed. by T. Gilby (New York, 1960), p. 312; Jaeger, *Paedeia,* trans. by G. Highet (New York, 1943), II, 64–65; Cornford, *Before and After Socrates* (Cambridge, 1932), p. 51.

[5] To my knowledge, only A. E. Taylor denies that Socrates meant to contradict the fact of moral weakness; in *Socrates* (New York, 1933), p. 133.

[6] Gomperz, *op. cit.,* II, 66–67.

[7] *The Development of Plato's Ethics* (Cambridge, 1955), p. 6.

[8] *Ibid.,* ch. i. Very briefly, Gould argues that the knowledge which Socrates thought sufficient for virtuous behavior is a form of "knowing how," a kind of moral ability comparable to the creative ability of the craftsmen. Professor Gregory Vlastos has shown, I believe, that this is not what Plato meant by "knowledge" in crucial cases such as "Courage is knowledge"; in "Socratic Knowledge and Platonic Pessimism," *Philosophical Review,* LXVI (1957), 227–232. Some considerations to the same effect are also produced by R. E. Allen, "The Socratic Paradox," *Journal of the History of Ideas,* XXI (1960).

## THE DISTINCTION BETWEEN THE PRUDENTIAL
## AND THE MORAL PARADOX

There is excellent textual evidence, at least in the *Gorgias* and the *Meno*, for drawing a sharp distinction between the two doctrines stated at the beginning of this paper. In the first place, Plato himself uses two distinct pairs of terms to state the two paradoxes. In the first paradox (and its corollary, that men desire only good things) he uses *agatha* (good things) and *kaka* (evil things), in the second *dikaia* (what is just) and *adika* (what is unjust). Moreover, there is an important difference in Plato's use of these two pairs of terms. The difference is as follows. Plato takes it for granted, and never argues, that *agatha* always benefit (*ofelein*) the possessor of them, and *kaka* always harm (*blabtein*) the possessor of them (for example, *Meno* 77d2–9, 87e; *Gorgias* 467a–b, 468b1–8). On the other hand, he *argues* that behaving justly (*dikaia prattein*) always benefits the agent, and that behaving unjustly always harms the agent; whether this is so, far from being taken for granted, is indeed the chief dispute between Socrates and Polus and Callicles, as Olympiodorus rightly points out.[9] A passage in the *Meno* 77d–e further suggests the difference: "Soc. And do you think that they know the evil things to be evil, those who think that such things benefit? Meno. I do not think that at all." The proposition that is being affirmed here with emphasis and not the least show of argument is that if someone thinks that something which is in fact evil benefits (the man who has or gets it) then he does not know that the thing is evil. To my knowledge Plato nowhere says, assumes, argues for, or implies that if a man thinks that something which is in fact unjust benefits (the agent) then he does not know that it is unjust. I shall say that for Plato it is in some sense definitional that *agatha* benefit whoever has them and that *kaka* harm; and I shall call this a prudential use of these terms. ("Evil" in view of these considerations becomes a poor translation of *kaka*, since the former word has moral connotations. I suggest as the least misleading translation "things good for one" for *agatha* and "things bad for one" for *kaka;* this now brings out the plausibility of supposing definitional connections with "benefit" and "harm.")[10]

---

[9] *In Platonis Gorgiam Commentaria*, ed. by W. Korvin (Lipsiae, 1936), p. 55.

[10] Generally, the neuters *agathon* and *kakon* have a prudential sense, though the story is quite different with the masculine and feminine forms; see, e.g.,

It results from these considerations that we cannot "lump together" the two doctrines and try to give the same account of both, as Cornford and others seem to do.[11] I shall call the first doctrine the prudential paradox, the second the moral paradox. The first is concerned with situations where no questions of justice and injustice (or, more generally, right and wrong) arise, and it appears to deny the fact of prudential weakness; the second is concerned with moral situations and appears to deny the fact of moral weakness.

## THE PRUDENTIAL PARADOX

In the course of refuting a definition of virtue proposed by Meno, Socrates offers what is the chief and yet much neglected argument for part of the prudential paradox, the argument that no one desires things that are bad for one. Socrates takes Meno's definition at 77b to imply that there are people who desire things that are bad for one, and Meno accepts this implication. Socrates immediately raises the question whether these people who, according to Meno, desire things that are bad for one, *know* that these things are bad for one or *think* that they are things good for one. Meno replies that there are people in both these classes, and Socrates now undertakes to show by a deduc-

---

A. W. H. Adkins, *Merit and Responsibility* (Oxford, 1960), pp. 30–31, 249–256. The neuter form is of course involved in every case of the prudential paradox. R. S. Bluck concurs that *kaka* is used in a prudential sense in the *Meno* 77–78 where the chief argument for the prudential paradox is given: *Plato's Meno* (Cambridge, 1961), p. 257. But he claims that by a fallacious argument "Plato is virtually making an assertion—that κακά must be harmful (in *some* way) to *all* concerned, *including the person who does the harm*" (Bluck's italics). In that argument, however, Plato neither assumes, nor does he need to, that *kaka* must be harmful to all concerned, but only that they are harmful to anyone who has (possesses, gets) them; moreover, that argument is not at all concerned with people who do harm, but only with people who, according to Meno, desire (to possess, get, have) *kaka*, knowing or not that they are *kaka*. In the *Meno* and the *Gorgias* it is fairly easy to distinguish between versions of the moral and prudential paradoxes, but unfortunately the situation in the *Protagoras* is not so clear cut. At 345d8–9, for instance, we seem to have a version of the prudential paradox, but two lines later we get a restatement of it in which *kaka* is coupled with *aischra*, a term that often, and probably here also, has moral connotations. More important, it is not entirely clear which paradox is involved in the well-known and difficult argument at 352b–358d4, and this is reflected in Professor Vlastos' treatment where both prudential and moral cases are given as counterexamples: *Plato's Protagoras* (New York, 1956), xliii, xliv. I think this argument makes far better sense if we suppose that it is concerned chiefly, if not entirely, with prudential situations; the language of the passage is heavily in favor of this, the only possible exception being 353c7 where *ponera* is used instead of *kaka*.

[11] Cornford, *op. cit.*, p. 51.

tive argument that both hypotheses are mistaken.[12] He begins arguing against the first hypothesis (there are people who desire things that are bad for one knowing that they are bad for one), interrupts this argument at 77d5–e4 in order to argue against the second hypothesis, and then resumes the argument against the first and concludes it at 78b. Instead of following this somewhat confusing procedure, I shall take up the argument against the first hypothesis, and then consider the much more difficult argument against the second.

Socrates' argument against the first hypothesis (itself the first premise in that argument which has the form of a *reductio*) is as follows: Meno agrees readily that desiring something is desiring to possess it,[13] and that a man who knows that a thing is bad for one also knows that it harms the one who has it. The people then who, according to Meno, desire bad things, knowing that they are bad, know that these things harm the one who has them and that they will be harmed by them (if they get them); they also think, Meno again agrees, that those who are harmed are miserable in proportion to the harm they suffer, and that the miserable are ill starred. (Hence, the men who, according to Meno, desire bad things knowing that they are bad desire to be miserable and ill starred.)[14] But, Meno agrees readily once more, no one wants (wishes) to be miserable and ill starred.[15] Hence, Socrates

[12] Unfortunately, Socrates' statement of the two hypotheses is faulty since they are exclusive but not exhaustive of the class of people who, according to Meno, desire bad things, unless we also suppose that the class of people who, according to Meno, desire bad things *thinking that they are good things* is the same as the class of people who desire bad things *not knowing that they are bad*. But it is not clear that Socrates could suppose this without begging the question.

[13] Τί ἐπιθυμεῖν λέγεις ; ἢ γενέσθαι αὐτῷ ; Γενέσθαι· τί γὰρ ἄλλο. We have exactly the same answers to similar questions at *Symp.* 204d5–7 and 204e2–4. For what may perhaps be regarded as grounds for this doctrine, see *Lysis* 221d–222, *Symp.* 200a2.

[14] This conclusion is not drawn in the text, but clearly it must be understood to follow from Meno's admissions so far, if his next admission—that no one wants to be miserable and ill starred—is to be relevant to the argument. Unfortunately, it is doubtful that this conclusion really follows: the argument has the form "If $S$ desires $X$ and knows that $X$ brings about $Y$, then $S$ desires $Y$"; it seems doubtful that an argument of this form is valid, since people may have conflicting desires.

[15] Up to this point in the argument Plato has used ἐπιθυμεῖν (to desire); now he introduces βούλεσθαι (to want, wish) and uses it for the rest of the argument. Scholars disagree as to whether the change is significant here, and generally whether in the dialogues different concepts correspond to the two words; cf., e.g., A. Croiset and L. Bodin, *Platon, Œuvres Complètes* (Paris, 1948), III, 245, and R. S. Bluck, *Plato's Meno* (Cambridge, 1961), p. 259. In point of fact, in addition to the definitions of βούλησις in *Definitions* 413c8–9, we have two pieces of explicit evidence that Plato has some important distinction between the two words:

finally concludes, no one (that is, no one of the people of the hypothesis) wants things that are bad for one if no one (whatsoever) wants to be miserable and ill starred.

To say that the passage in which Socrates argues against the second hypothesis is problematic is an understatement. This hypothesis, at 77c2–3, is that there are some people who desire bad things thinking (mistakenly, presumably) that they are good things; to this it may be added, as a result of what is agreed at 77d3–7, that these people do not know that these things (which they desire) are bad. The problematic passage runs as follows:

Obviously they do not desire bad things, the people who are ignorant of them, but [they desire] the things which they supposed to be good things, even though these things are in fact bad; so that those who are ignorant of them and think them good really desire good things. Isn't that so? Meno. It would seem to be so in their case.[16]

There are at least three problems here: (1) To see how Socrates can claim *consistently* both that these people do not desire bad things and also that they desire things which they thought to be good though *these things are in fact bad* (one might be tempted to infer from Soc-

---

*Charmides* 167e1–6 clearly implies, it seems to me, that the object of every desire (ἐπιθυμία) is a pleasure, and the object of every wish (βούλησις) is a good, and of course Plato holds that some pleasures are bad for one; and in *Lysis* 221a7–b3 we are told that the satisfaction of desires sometimes will benefit one and other times will harm, and two lines later it is implied that there are such things as bad desires (κακαί ἐπιθυμίαι), whereas Plato never speaks, to my knowledge, of bad or harmful βούλησις. Using the terminology that I introduce below (p. 155), the distinction suggested by these two passages, can be stated as follows: In no case can the *intended* object of a desire (ἐπιθυμία) be a bad thing, but the *actual* object can be, and often is, a bad thing; whereas in the case of wish (βούλησις), neither the intended nor the actual object of wish can ever be a bad thing. This distinction is consistent with Plato's use in the present argument, where he uses βούλεσθαι to deny Meno's claim that there are people who desire bad things knowing that they are bad, and ἐπιθυμεῖν to deny the claim that there are people who desire what are in fact bad things not knowing that they are bad; his using ἐπιθυμεῖν in the latter case allows us to interpret the denial as not including a denial that the actual objects of these people's desires are bad things. Interpreted in this way, Socrates' denial of the second hypothesis is consistent with the view in the *Lysis* and elsewhere that some desires are bad or harmful.

16 Where Lamb has "evil" and "good," I have "bad things" and "good things"; we have the neuter plural in the text throughout this passage. The expressions in brackets have been supplied by me. Croiset and Bodin go as far as to translate Socrates' last sentence as *de sorte qu'*en desirant ce mal *qu'ils ne connaissent pas*"; I think this is correct *as an interpretation*, but there is certainly nothing in the text that corresponds to the phrase I have emphasized.

rates' last two claims that these people do desire bad things, and say that Socrates contradicted himself within the space of three lines). (2) To see on what grounds Socrates can assert the first of these statements. And (3) to see how Socrates can plausibly infer, as he seems to do, that these people really desire good things (not simply things they *thought* to be good).

The key to the solution of these problems and to a sound interpretation of the passage lies in the fact that statements of desire, wish, want ("He desires . . .") are cases of indirect discourse. A statement such as "He desired to be the first European to land on the new continent" *may* change in truth value if we substitute "the first European to be killed by Indians" for "the first European to land on the new continent" even though these two expressions in fact refer to one and the same person (and similarly with expressions of the form "an *f*" or "*F* things" when substituted for coextensive expressions).[17] It follows that Socrates is in no danger of contradicting himself when he asserts that the people in the hypothesis desire what they thought to be good things, that these things are in fact bad things, and yet that these people do not desire bad things.

What lies behind the fact that statements of desire, among others, are cases of indirect discourse is that, as Frege puts it, "a conviction or a belief is the ground of a feeling";[18] if a man desires something, it is his conception of what the object is that is the ground of his desire, not (necessarily) what the object in fact is (he may be under a misconception as to what sort of thing the object is or unaware that it has a certain property). If, then, a man reaches for something—say the salt shaker—does not express reservations or show reluctance in doing so, and we say "He wants the salt shaker," we might, even under these conditions, be misdescribing the object of his desire (want): misdescribing not in the sense that "salt shaker" is not applicable to the object he reaches for, but in the sense that "salt shaker" is not the description *under which* he desires it (this would turn out to be the case if the man was not aware that what he was reaching for was a salt shaker or if, for example, he mistook the salt shaker for the pepper

---

[17] Frege lists several other cases where words are used indirectly or have their indirect reference: "On Sense and Reference," in *Translations from the Writings of Gottlob Frege*, ed. by P. Geach and M. Black (Oxford, 1952), pp. 66 ff. For more recent discussions, see, e.g., W. and M. Kneale, *The Development of Logic* (Oxford, 1962), pp. 601–618, and W. V. O. Quine, *Word and Object* (New York, 1960), pp. 151–156.

[18] *Op. cit.*, p. 67.

mill).[19] It seems then that we ought to say that a statement of the form "He desires (wants) . . ." is not to count as true unless the description that fills the blank is the description under which the object is desired; I shall call such a description the description of the *intended* object of desire. At the same time, this is compatible with regarding a certain kind of behavior toward an object and our knowledge of the object as reasonable evidence for saying that someone desires so-and-so; thus, if a man reaches for (goes after, aims at) something, does not show reservations or reluctance in doing so, and what he is reaching for is, for example, a salt shaker, then we have reasonable evidence for saying (claiming) that he wants the salt shaker.[20] But of course we must remember that when such is our evidence for making the statement, we run the risk of misdescribing the object of the man's desire; to mark this point, I shall say that when a statement of the form "He desires (wants) . . ." is made on such evidence, the description that fills the blank is the description of the *actual* object of desire. It is clear that one and the same description could be the description of both the intended and the actual object of desire. It is also clear that there is no contradiction in saying, for example, both that the intended object of the man's desire was the pepper mill and that the actual object of his desire was the salt shaker.[21]

19 I have taken this phrase from Anscombe, *Intention* (Oxford, 1958), p. 65. It may be asked, how can we tell when a description is the description under which something is desired (wanted)? One way is to ask the man what he wants or to see how he asks for what he wants; if a man says (to the grocer) "I want a loaf of wheat bread," it is under the description "loaf of wheat bread" that he wants to buy what the grocer brings him. It is worth noting that if a man wants something, which is in fact *F*, and the man knows that it is *F*, this is necessary but not sufficient for concluding that it is under the description *F* that the man wants it. For it may not be the case that he wants it *qua F;* he may be indifferent to its being *F*.

20 That we have reasonable evidence for saying so is compatible with changing our minds on the basis of subsequent behavior (e.g., his showing surprise when salt pours out of the object he got).

21 I have already switched from "description of intended object" to "intended object." It may be asked what the intended object of desire is. Suppose, e.g., (1) Jones wants a loaf of wheat bread (in the sense that "loaf of wheat bread" is the description of the intended object of his desire). What is the intended object of Jones's desire? It is not, of course, the description "loaf of wheat bread"—that would be absurd. Now why can't we give the obvious answer: the intended object of his desire is a loaf of wheat bread? It is sometimes held that this obvious answer is mistaken on the ground that it is possible for (1) to be true even though it is also true that (2) there are not in fact any loaves of wheat bread. This objection is very puzzling; I can understand it only on the supposition that the objector assumes that (3) if someone desires something, then there is something which is desired. But this seems to me a complete mistake. I do not

Now in the passage we are considering, we can say that what Socrates is denying is that bad things are the *intended* objects of these people's desires. For his only basis in the passage for saying that the people in the hypothesis do not desire bad things is the statement that these people do not know that the things, which according to Meno they desire, are bad; and the only relevant statement that follows from this is that bad things are not the intended objects of their desires. Further, the only basis that Socrates has in this passage for saying that the people in the hypothesis really desire good things is the statement that they thought that the things, which according to Meno they desire, were good things; and the only relevant thing that can follow from this is that good things are the *intended* objects of their desires (at any rate if they desire these things, which according to Meno they desire, because they think they are good things or *qua* good things). It is important to realize that Socrates is not denying (he certainly does not have to) that the actual objects of these people's desires are indeed bad things; his statement, that "these things (which they thought to be good things) are in fact bad," is good enough evidence for this, and, in addition, it is not part of his case that these people express reluctance or show reservations in pursuing (going after) things which are in fact bad. (On this see also footnote 15.)

I am not of course claiming that Socrates (or Plato) was aware of the distinction between direct and indirect discourse on which the present interpretation is based. In this regard, all that can be safely inferred is that, unlike Meno, Socrates is unwilling to say that a man who pursues bad things desires bad things unless the man is aware that they are bad. In this Socrates is clearly correct, provided we do not take his unwillingness as a denial that the actual objects of some people's desires are bad things.

In sum, we can say (using the terminology introduced) that what Socrates has tried to show is that in no case are bad things the intended objects of people's desires, though in some cases they are the actual objects. In his arguments he has used three crucial premises, all readily agreed to by Meno without argument: that desiring something

---

know of what logical form (1) is, but the fact that both (1) and (2) can be true at once shows conclusively, it seems to me, that (1) is not of the form $(\exists x)$ ($x$ is a loaf of bread. Jones desires $x$). And if (3) says anything at all, it says that (1) has this form. The fact that (1) and (2) can both be true, far from being an objection to the obvious answer, shows that the above objection is mistaken. I do not see, therefore, that, in order to say correctly "The intended object of Jones's desire is such and such," the such and such must exist.

is desiring to possess it; that if one knows or believes that a thing is bad for one, he also knows or believes that it harms the man who has it and in proportion to the harm makes him miserable; and that no one desires to be miserable (in the sense that to be miserable is never the intended object of anyone's desire). Of these only the last is even a plausible candidate for a factual proposition, a proposition that is supposed to represent a general fact concerning "human nature."[22] It is far from obvious that this proposition contradicts any facts; indeed it, or some version of it, seems to be one of the most common presuppositions made in accounting for human behavior, at any rate in situations of prudential choice. If anyone supposes that the prudential paradox contradicts facts because it is based on this proposition, the burden of proof is on him, not on Plato.

### THE MORAL PARADOX

In the moral paradox we have two propositions: virtue is knowledge, and all who do injustice do so involuntarily. I shall concentrate on the first of these, and interpret the second in terms of it. The first is usually interpreted as a biconditional: if one has knowledge one is virtuous; if one is virtuous one has knowledge. Most commentators take "knowledge" to mean "knowledge of virtue," so that the first part of the biconditional becomes "If one has knowledge of virtue one is a virtuous man." It is plausible enough to take the contrapositive of this to mean that if a man does something that is unjust (or intemperate, cowardly, or the like), then he does not know that it is unjust. And if it is a familiar, or even rare, fact of experience that men sometimes do injustice or wrong knowing that they are doing so, we do seem to have here a Platonic doctrine that contradicts facts. The strongest single piece of evidence for this interpretation is in the *Gorgias* 460b–d. Here, Socrates asserts that "he who has learnt what is just is a just man"; he then proceeds to make matters worse by adding that the just man always does what is just and never even desires to do what is unjust. This position seems to be even more extraordinary than the previous one, since it seems to deny also the fact that sometimes men have morally bad desires (that is, the fact that sometimes to do injustice or wrong is the *intended* object of man's desires).

---

[22] ἐν ἀνθρώπου φύσει, *Prot.* 358d1–2. If I am right in thinking that the argument here is confined to prudential situations (see note 8), it should not be supposed that Plato is saying here that it is not in human nature to wish to do wrong—an extraordinary proposition indeed.

I want to take as the main guide for the interpretation of the moral paradox the fact that it can be derived from three doctrines that Plato certainly holds. There is evidence that in the *Gorgias* Plato himself derives part of the paradox from these doctrines.

The first of these is the prudential paradox itself. The second is the view that no action (or, at any rate, no unjust or wrong action) is ever done for its own sake and that every action (or, at any rate, every unjust or wrong action) is done for the sake of possessing what the agent considers a good—that is, something beneficial to himself.[23] Finally, we need for the derivation of the moral paradox the well-known Platonic doctrine, argued in the *Gorgias* (and of course in the *Republic*), that doing what is just (and, more generally, right) always benefits the agent, and doing what is unjust always harms the agent; and consequently, that it is always better for the agent to do justice rather than injustice no matter what the circumstances.

I have given only a bare outline of the last two doctrines, but this is sufficient for my present purposes.

Consider now the most problematic part of the moral paradox: if one has knowledge, one is virtuous (or, knowledge is a sufficient condition for being virtuous). The basic difference between the traditional interpretation and the one I am about to suggest turns on what we take "knowledge" to include and on the distinction between the items included in this knowledge. The traditional interpretation is that Plato meant "knowledge of virtue," so that the paradoxical statement becomes "If one knows what is virtuous, one will do what is virtuous."[24] I suggest, on the other hand, that Plato meant that if a man has knowledge of what is virtuous and *also* knowledge that it is always better for one to do what is virtuous, then he will always (so long as he has this knowledge and virtuous behavior is in his power) behave virtuously. I

---

[23] The whole argument with Polus, *Gorg.* 466b–470c, presupposes this doctrine, which is stated explicitly at 467c–468e. See also *Symp.* 181a–b, 182e–183b; C. Ritter, *The Essence of Plato's Thought* (New York, 1933), pp. 41, 53; P. Shorey, *What Plato Said* (Chicago, 1933), p. 139; E. R. Dodds, *Plato, Gorgias* (Oxford, 1959), p. 235.

[24] There is of course no universal agreement on this. Some writers seem to suppose that it is knowledge of one's own good: see, e.g., A. M. Adam, *Plato* (Cambridge, 1913), p. 15. This is as much of a mistake as the interpretation I am criticizing. Even if virtuous behavior is always to one's own good and wrong behavior always harmful to the agent, it does not follow that knowledge of one's own good presupposes knowledge of this proposition or knowledge of what is virtuous or wrong behavior. Knowledge of one's own good can be sufficient, at most, for behavior that is to one's own good.

suggest, further, that these two items of knowledge are logically independent, in the sense that a man may have one without having the
other.

The first advantage of this interpretation is that the Platonic
thesis, that knowledge is sufficient for virtue, no longer contradicts the
fact of moral weakness. The thesis is that if a man knows what is virtuous (and what is not) and also knows that it is always better for one
to behave virtuously, then he will always do what is virtuous and will
not even desire to do otherwise. What follows from this is that if a
man commits injustice (or behaves in a cowardly or intemperate fashion), then he does not know either that he is committing injustice or
that doing so is worse for him or both. It is clear that this proposition
does not contradict the proposition that sometimes men do what is
unjust (or wrong) knowing or believing that it is unjust. Hence, on
this interpretation the main reason for thinking Plato's thesis paradoxical is removed.

The second advantage of this interpretation is that the moral paradox does really now follow from the three doctrines stated earlier.
These doctrines are that men desire (to possess, to get) only good
things (in the sense explained above), that they do what they do not
for its own sake but for the sake of possessing good things, and that
justice (and, more generally, virtuous behavior) always benefits the
agent whereas injustice harms him. It follows that if a man knows
which actions are just (and which unjust) and also knows that it is
always better for him to do justice rather than injustice, then he will
desire to do what is just, and will do what is just (in the relevant situations) unless this is not in his power. If a man who had such knowledge
desired to do injustice, this would imply that he desired to possess a
bad thing, which contradicts the prudential paradox. The *Gorgias* provides evidence that Plato himself based the moral paradox on the three
doctrines stated earlier. At 509e, where Socrates asserts a related part
of the moral paradox—that no one does injustice willingly, but that all
who do injustice do so involuntarily[25]—he explicitly cites as the basis

---

[25] μηδένα βουλόμενον ἀδικεῖν, ἀλλ'ἄκοντας τοὺς ἀδικοῦντας πάντας ἀδικεῖν.
"Willingly" and "involuntarily" may be bad translations. If we place this proposition in its proper context (the discussion with Polus), it is clear that Plato does
not mean that these people act reluctantly or with reservations or that they are
forced to do injustice; he means that they act in ignorance that what they do is
unjust or harmful to them or both. And if the corresponding knowledge, together with the universal desire for things that are good for one, is sufficient for
acting justly, this implies that the people in question would not have acted unjustly, and would not have wanted to, if they had this knowledge. This gives

for this his discussion with Polus. And what he and Polus agreed on, in the main, were the doctrines in question: that men desire only good things, that men do what they do not for its own sake but because they think it is better for them, and that doing what is just is not only honorable or fair, but also good for the agent (whereas injustice is harmful). In addition, it is worth noting that when Polus brings up examples of extreme wrong-doers such as Archelaus, the dispute is not whether this man knew or believed that what he did was unjust (indeed, this issue never comes up!), but whether he was better off doing injustice, as he himself believed. This suggests that one explanation that Plato would give as to why people do wrong is that they do not know that it is worse for them. Of course, on the interpretation that is presented here Plato can give either one or both of two general explanations as to why people do wrong (when they are not forced to): that they do not know that it is wrong, or that they do not know it is worse for them; whereas on the interpretation I am criticizing, only the first of these explanations is available to Plato.

I do not see, on the other hand, how the moral paradox, on the traditional interpretation, can be derived from Platonic doctrines: we are to suppose that knowledge that an action is just (or temperate, or courageous, and so forth) is sufficient for doing it (in the relevant situations) and even for desiring to do it. I do not think this proposition can be derived from Platonic doctrines. Plato argues, in effect, that there is a necessary connection between recognizing something as good for one and desiring (to have, to get, to possess) it; but he does not argue nor does he hold, in my opinion, that there is a necessary connection between recognizing an action as just and desiring to do it.

It may be objected that on Plato's view knowledge that an action is just (or unjust) presupposes a knowledge of justice (and injustice), and that the latter presupposes a knowledge that it is always better for one to behave justly rather than unjustly; so that it could not be the case that a man had knowledge that an action is just and at the same time did not know that it was to his greater advantage to do it. It would follow from this that though both items are included in the knowledge that is sufficient for virtuous behavior, as I have suggested, they are nevertheless not logically independent.

There is some evidence that Plato holds that if a man knows the

---

some plausibility to saying that these people act unwillingly or involuntarily, though of course it remains doubtful at best that acting involuntarily in this sense can exempt one from blame (see *Nic. Ethics* 1110b).

definition of justice in a man (justice in a man being a state of soul characterized by a certain kind of order and, perhaps, harmony), he cannot fail to see that it is always better for one to be in this state of soul rather than any other (see, for example, Glaucon's reply at *Rep.* 445a–c after justice in the soul has been defined). But it does not follow from this, nor is it Plato's doctrine, that in order to know that an *action* is just one has to know the definition of justice in the soul. In the *Rep.* 443, for example, Plato says that the definition of justice in the soul may be confirmed by "commonplace and vulgar tests of justice"; this implies that there are "commonplace and vulgar" standards of justice by which a man may know, for example, that it is unjust to embezzle gold that has been entrusted to him, without knowing the definition of justice in the soul. I suggest then that on Plato's view knowing or believing that an action is just is logically independent of knowing or believing that just actions benefit the agent and unjust ones harm him. And this is quite consistent with what I take to be also his view: that just actions necessarily benefit the agent and unjust ones necessarily harm him.

Incidentally, it cannot be taken for granted that Plato means to exclude the view that true *belief* (as distinct from knowledge) is sufficient for acting justly. Though he uses *sofia, episteme, mathesis* (all usually translated "knowledge"), which he distinguishes from *pistis* or *doxa* (belief, opinion), in stating the moral paradox, he nevertheless contrasts these with ignorance or false belief (never with true belief) when he argues for the moral paradox.[26] It is reasonable to suppose that he would accept the view that true belief (that an action is just and it is also to one's advantage or greater advantage to do it), if it is a firm conviction, would be sufficient for acting justly. It is even reasonable to suppose that *false* belief, if it is a firm conviction, would be sufficient for acting *in accordance with the belief*, though of course it may not be sufficient for acting justly; at any rate it is difficult to see how the arguments given for knowledge would not apply here.

It is important to emphasize that on the interpretation I have suggested the condition that is sufficient for virtuous behavior includes not only knowledge but also the *desire* for things that are good for one (and the consequent desire to do always what is beneficial or more beneficial for oneself). This point emerged from the way I have de-

---

[26] *Prot.* 360b–c, 360d1–2. The argument here provides ample evidence also that the wisdom that is sufficient for being courageous includes knowledge of what is better for one.

rived the moral paradox, and it is worth emphasizing because it is sometimes thought that Plato did not see that there is a "gap," as it were, between knowledge and action; that, no matter what knowledge a man has, his desires and passions may prompt him to act against this knowledge. It is to take care of this very point that Plato argues that no man desires things that are bad for one, that men desire only good things, and that they do what they do for the sake of what they consider a benefit to themselves. Part of the reason this point is not usually emphasized in discussions of the Socratic paradoxes may be the fact that Plato holds that this desire is common to all men, whether virtuous or wrong-doers, and hence that what accounts for the difference between them is not presence or absence of this desire, but of knowledge. This is quite true; but is also consistent with saying, as I am saying, that this doctrine of desire—what may be called an egoistic theory of motivation—is essential to the moral paradox. The form in which the paradox is usually stated—that virtue is knowledge or that knowledge is sufficient for being virtuous—is misleading in this respect: in considering it, one tends to forget the doctrine of desire or motivation that underlies it. But what Plato is saying is that, *given* this universal desire for possessing (having, getting) things that are good for one, *then* knowledge of virtue and vice and knowledge that it is always to one's greater advantage to behave virtuously is sufficient for such behavior.

It seems to me then that traditional accounts of the paradoxes have gone wrong in either one or both of two ways. In the first place, it was not always seen or properly emphasized that the doctrine of desire—what I have called Plato's egoistic theory of motivation—is part of the logical foundation of the moral paradox; and consequently it has seemed as if Plato ignored the role of desires and passions in the choice of right or wrong behavior and thought that this choice depended entirely on knowledge. If I am right, the truth of the matter is that Plato considered the central desire for the possession of things that are good for one as absolutely essential in any account of human behavior. If Plato has gone wrong at all in this, it may be in the strong emphasis he seems to place on the dependence of one's desires and passions on one's convictions, and in the fact that he writes, in the early dialogues at least, as if there is no stronger desire or passion than this central desire for things that are good for one (or, perhaps more plausibly, the desire for one's own happiness). In the second place, it was not always seen or properly emphasized that the Platonic doctrine that virtuous behavior is always more beneficial to the agent than wrong behavior is also part of the logical foundation of the moral paradox;

and consequently it was not seen that there is, at the very least, a possibility that on Plato's view the knowledge which, together with the desire, is sufficient for virtuous behavior includes two items that, as items of knowledge, are logically independent. On this possibility, as we have seen, the moral paradox does not deny the fact of moral weakness.

The interpretation I have sketched seems to me to constitute a resolution of the Socratic paradoxes in so far as it removes the two elements that traditionally have been the most puzzling—the extreme intellectualism and the alleged denial of moral weakness—and in so far as it renders, as I think it does, Plato's account of the relation of knowledge to conduct (a relation that is now mediated by the element of desire) far more plausible than it is usually supposed to be. But it is not, of course, part of my contention that the Socratic paradoxes are true, nor do I consider showing this part of such a resolution. I have not shown, nor attempted to show, that the paradoxes do not contradict any facts, but only that they do not contradict what they are usually supposed to contradict. Nor have I claimed that the doctrines from which the paradoxes are derived are true, especially the doctrine that it is always to one's own greater advantage to do justice rather than injustice. If this doctrine is false, as it appears to be, then no one can have the knowledge or *true* opinion that Plato thought sufficient (together with the desire) for virtuous conduct. Nevertheless, even if the Socratic paradoxes are partly false, they deserve the great attention they have received. The relation of knowledge to conduct is not only of theoretical interest but also of great importance to the political reformer; for one's concepts of moral education and punishment turn on one's conception of that relation.

# SOCRATIC DEFINITION*

## Richard Robinson

## § 1. THE WHAT-IS-X? QUESTION

The Socrates of Plato's dialogues is continually asking questions. Let us distinguish these into the primary question and the secondary questions. In each discussion he first proposes some important problem, usually ethical; and that is the primary question. As soon as an answer is suggested, he proceeds to examine it by means of a series of questions to the answerer; and those are the secondary questions. This chapter is concerned only with Socrates' primary questions.

These primary questions have, roughly speaking, one of two forms: either "Is X Y?" or "What is X?" Examples of "Is X Y?" are: "Is justice better than injustice?" in the *Republic*, "Are those who become friends like each other?" in the *Lysis*, and "Ought Socrates to escape?" in the *Crito*. Examples of "What is X?" are: "What is justice?" in the *Republic*, "What is temperance?" in the *Charmides*, and "What is courage?" in the *Laches*. Of these two types it is the What-is-X? form that stands out and catches the attention of every student of Plato's early dialogues. This is not, apparently, because there is actually more space devoted to the discussion of What-is-X? questions than to the other type; for only three or four of the early dialogues are primarily and directly engaged in such discussion throughout their philosophical parts, namely the *Euthyphro*, the *Laches*, the *Charmides*, and the *Hippias Major*. The *Gorgias*, the *Meno*, and *Republic* I (which we may count an early dialogue) all abandon the question "What is X?" for the question "Is X Y?"; while the *Ion*, the *Hippias Minor*, the *Apology*, the *Crito*, and the *Protagoras*, never raise the question at all. The explicit question of the *Lysis* is not what friendship is but what its condition is, although the former question is present as a faint undercurrent, and there is perhaps some confusion between the two. The

* From *Plato's Earlier Dialectic* by Richard Robinson, 2nd edition (Oxford, 1953), pp. 49–60. Reprinted by permission of the Clarendon Press, Oxford.

What-is-X? question therefore owes its prominence in the early dialogues not to spatial predominance but to the emphasis which Socrates puts upon it.

Socrates often expresses dissatisfaction with the answer he receives to his What-is-X? question, on the ground not that it is false but that it is not the *kind* of answer he had in mind when he asked "What is X?" Thus in the *Theaetetus* (146), which in this respect is just like an early dialogue, Socrates, having asked "What is knowledge?" and been told that it is geometry and shoemaking and so on, replies that he asked for one and has been given many. "You were not asked what things there is knowledge of, nor how many sorts of knowledge there are; for our aim in asking was not to count the sorts of knowledge but to know what knowledge itself is." He then gives an illustration of the kind of answer he wants: if he had asked "What is clay?" he would have wanted, not a list of the various sorts of clay, but simply "earth mixed with liquid" (147C). In this explanation there are two key phrases that Socrates uses to indicate his desire. One is the opposition between the "one" and the "many"; he wants the one knowledge and not the many knowledges. The other is "what X itself is." These phrases constantly recur when Socrates is talking about his What-is-X? question.

He explains his question at length in the *Meno* (71–77). Here also he gives examples of the sort of answer he requires: if he asked "What is figure?" a good answer would be "the limit of a solid" (76A). Here also he uses the opposition of the one and the many (77A): he explains that he wants not some virtue but virtue (73E), that which is the same in all the Xes (75A). The *Meno* also has two other ways which are of great importance to Socrates in explaining the nature of his question. One is the use of the word εἶδος or form; he wants, he says, "some one identical form possessed by all the virtues, through which they are virtues, to which the answerer ought to look in explaining to the asker what virtue really is" (72C, cf. *Euthyph.* 6D). The other way of explaining the question is by means of the word οὐσία or being or essence; when he says "What is X?" he wants the being or essence of X (72B, cf. *Euthyph.* 11A).

Socrates frequently asserts that the question What is X? is prior to certain other questions about X, in the sense that we cannot find sure answers to those other questions until we have found sure answers to this one. You cannot, he says, know what *sort* of thing X is until you know *what* X is. Thus you cannot really know whether virtue is teachable until you know what virtue is (*Men.* 71, 86DE, 100B; *Prt.*

360E), nor whether justice is a virtue until you know what justice is (*Rp.* I 354C). You must also know what X is before you can know whether it is beneficial (*Rp.* I 354C and *La.* 189E–190A), or how it is to be obtained (cf. *La.* 189E–190A and all the passages on the teachability of virtue). The most surprising of all his assertions in this line is that at the end of the *Lysis:* "Well, said I, we have become ridiculous, Lysis and Menexenus, both I who am old and you. For as these people go away they will say that we think we are friends of each other—for I count myself among you—but we have not yet been able to discover what a friend is." This is surprising because it seems to imply that until you know what X is you can never say whether this is a case of X. That our knowledge of X is prior to our knowledge of its cases is implied also in the *Euthyphro* (6E), where Socrates says that when Euthyphro has told him what X is he is going to use it as a paradigm or pattern to determine which things are X and which not. In fact, the impression vaguely given by the early dialogues as a whole is that Socrates thinks that there is no truth whatever about X that can be known before we know what X is. He never explicitly says so; nor, on the other hand, does he ever set any limits to the priority of this question. Prior to ascertaining what X is, he seems to think, we can form more or less probable opinions that X, whatever it may be, possesses the character Y, but can never be certain of such a thing (cf. *Tht.* 196DE).

Nor does Plato represent Socrates as seeking to answer his What-is-X? question by looking to cases or examples of X. On the contrary, as we have seen, he makes Socrates rebuke those answerers who give him some of the many Xes instead of the one X itself. Only when an answer of the desired sort is already given does anything like a case appear in the Socratic discussions; and then it is used not to establish but to refute the proposed answer.

If we look in the early dialogues for justifications of this principle, for reasons why the question What is X? must always be answered prior to any other question about X, we do not find them. On the contrary, the principle is offered as self-evident and too obvious for discussion. There is, however, something like an argument to this point in the mature *Phaedrus* (260). Imagine, says Socrates, that I were to urge you to use a horse in war, while neither of us was acquainted with horses, but I knew that you thought a horse to be that domestic animal which has the longest ears. This would be absurd. But it is like what actually happens in cities, for ignorant orators persuade ignorant cities to do bad things, both parties being under the impression that they are good things. Before you can say anything useful about horses you must know what a horse is; and before you can say anything useful about the good you must know what the good is. A twentieth-century philosopher would reply that it is a matter of experience that we can and do make useful statements about X without being able to say what X is in the way Socrates desires; and therefore the above argument must conceal some false premiss or fallacious inference.

The presentation of the What-is-X? question in Plato's early dialogues is no more abstract than I have represented it above. If we describe it, as I have so far refrained from doing, by means of such words as "definition" and "example," if we extract from it explicit rules and principles of definition, we pass to a stage of abstraction higher than the dialogues themselves display. We can, indeed, pick out an occasional word to be appropriately translated by "example" or "definition," and we can very easily formulate, from Socrates' instructions to his hearers, rules resembling those in a modern textbook; but that is only to say that each level of abstraction is near to the next! The actual picture in the dialogues is not more but less abstract than the picture here given; for Socrates does not use the letter X; he never gives the function but always one of its arguments.

Throughout the long series of his dialogues Plato continued to believe in the propriety and importance of this search for essences which he had depicted at the beginning of his writings. He can laugh at himself from time to time, and represent the demand for the "one" instead of the "many" as a piece of sophistical perversity (*Sph.* 239E–240A); but it remained his own demand. It is what he refers to as "taking the logos of the essence" (*Rp.* 534B) or simply "giving a logos." It came to seem to him much more difficult than he had at first assumed it to be (*Letters* VII, 342–3, is one of his most despondent discussions of it); and he was thus led to spend much thought on devising methods to accomplish it. The great theory of dialectic is the theory of the method of discovering essence. Especially is this so in the *Sophist* and later dialogues, when the instrument of dialectic was division; for the purpose of division was precisely to give the definition of the essence. It is somewhat less so in the middle dialogues; for the method of hypothesis, which is the form dialectic takes there, is not so much a way of discovering essence as a way of evading the search for essence while still paying lip-service to the principle that you cannot know anything else about X until you know what X *is*. At least this seems to be the purpose of the method of hypothesis in its first appearance, which is in the *Meno*. The problem of that dialogue is whether virtue is teachable. Socrates declares that to answer we must first ascertain what virtue *is*. The attempt to ascertain this fails, however; and rather than abandon the discussion they are led to *hypothesize* a certain account of the essence of virtue and consider whether it would be teachable on this assumption (87).

Repeated failures in the effort to discover any particular essence only increased Plato's eagerness and his certainty that the essences were there. He thus came to introduce an element not found in the early dialogues at all, namely reflection on *essence in general, or the essences as a body*, as opposed to concentrating always on one particular essence; and these reflections are what is called Plato's theory of Ideas.

## § 2. CRITIQUE OF THE WHAT-IS-X? QUESTION

If we now cease to confine ourselves to something like English translations of Plato's words, and make use of modern terms and higher abstractions in order to criticize the What-is-X? question, the first thing we notice is that Socrates is looking for equivalences. He wants an answer, say "X is AB," such that every X is AB and nothing else is AB. If given an answer, such as "X is A," where A is not equivalent to but broader than X, he points out that other things besides X are A, and asks to have marked off the part of A that is equivalent to X (e.g. *Prt.* 312; *Grg.* 449 ff., 453C ff.).

There are, however, various sorts of equivalence or convertible proposition; and it appears that Socrates is not ready to accept any kind. In the first place, there are verbal definitions, such as "*Hund* means dog." Socrates does not want these. He is not asking for a dictionary-definition of some word previously unknown to him. On the contrary, the X in his questions is always some word which he and his companions use every day of their lives, some word which, in unphilosophical circles, they would be said to know the meaning of perfectly well. Thus, while, in the ordinary sense, he knows what the word X means (and what it means is surely the thing X), he nevertheless does not know what the thing X is. Yet he expects the answer to his question to be itself a set of words. It seems, therefore, that his procedure implies, though he was unaware of it, that there is a word or set of words, which gives or enshrines a knowledge of the thing X in some way in which the word X does not enshrine a knowledge of the thing X even for those who understand it and use it correctly. If the desired answer is "X is AB," then, although he understands the word X just as well as the words AB, and although they both indicate the same entity, yet when he has the whole phrase "X is AB" he knows satisfactorily what that entity is, and when he only has the word X he does not.

Any equivalent of X may serve as a means by which someone identifies X or distinguishes it from something else; but, among such equivalents, some, as we vaguely say, "give the essence of X" and others do not. It is possible to identify X without giving its essence, by making use of other elements of reality and their relation to X. The proposition that "virtue is the only human character which can never be misused" identifies virtue by referring to human character and misuse; and it evidently does not give its essence. It simply gives virtue a unique place in the context of reality, as two numbers give a point a unique place in a system of plane coordinates. Every statement giving X's essence serves to identify X; but not every statement serving to identify X gives its essence.

Now will Socrates be satisfied with any sort of identification, or does he insist on an identification through essence? The answer is that he has not made this distinction, and speaks sometimes one way and sometimes the other.

On the one hand, many passages suggest that all he wants is a mark that shall serve as a pattern by which to judge of any given thing whether it is an X or not. In the *Euthyphro* (6E) he describes his aim in just this way. In the *Meno* (74BC) he gives the fact that there are figures other than roundness as the reason why roundness is a bad description of figure. In the same dialogue (75B) he offers the following as an example of the kind of answer he wants: "Figure is that which alone of all things invariably accompanies colour." This is clearly nothing more than a designation or identification; and, though Meno objects to it, he does so on the ground not that it ought to be more than a designation but that it would not identify the thing for a person for whom the word "figure" by itself did not already do the business. The same purpose is suggested again by Socrates' habit of illustrating his What-is-X? question by cases where X is an individual (*Men.* 71B, *Tht.* 209, *Grg.* 453C); for surely a convertible proposition about an individual cannot be more than an identification. It is suggested again by a word he often uses to describe the process of answering a What-is-it? question, namely ὁρίζειν. For this term, never losing the feel of its original connexion with boundary-stones, suggests laying down a mark to distinguish a field from the next, without in any way describing the soils or the crops in the fields so delimited. And in

Plato's dialogues the translations "distinguish" and "determine" are suitable as often or more often than "define."

In many other passages, however, Socrates' purpose in asking What is X? is evidently not, or not merely, to distinguish X from everything else. It is to get at what he calls the essence or the form of X, the one in the many, that single identical something whose presence in all the many Xes is guaranteed precisely by the fact that we call them all Xes (*Men.* 74D).

There is thus a duality in Socrates' conception of the question What is X? On the one hand it is merely the search for an equivalent of X, for any description convertible therewith. On the other hand, it is the search for something felt to be narrower than this, for one special equivalent of X which is felt to be X in a more intimate way than any of the others.

There is a curious trace of this duality in the *Theaetetus*. The last ten pages of that dialogue contain a rather careful discussion of the conception of logos, and distinguish three meanings of the word. The first of these meanings is the expression of a thought in words. Now Aristotle often narrowed this meaning of logos down to the expression in words of a thought that gives a definition. Logos thus came to mean the formula of a definition, the description that gives the essence; and this is prepared by a passage in the *Republic* (534B), where Plato says that the dialectician takes the logos of the essence of each thing. In this sense, then, logos means the expression of an answer to the question What is X? The interesting point is that Plato's other two senses of logos in the *Theaetetus* appear to reflect the two ways in which Socrates regards the What-is-X? question in the early dialogues. According to one of these senses the logos is that in which the thing differs from all other things; here we have clearly the notion of the What-is-X? question as the effort to differentiate and distinguish. The notion of it as a search for essence is reflected in the other sense, according to which the logos of X is a statement of the elements of X; for that the essence of a thing is to be found in its elements is a notion that always arises when the search for essence is pushed very far.

Socrates almost invariably assumes that his term X is univocal. He has no fear of ambiguity. Since you call all these things by one name, he says, tell me what is the one thing you mean every time (*Men.* 74D). "We are accustomed to posit some one form for each set of things to which we apply the same name" (*Rp.* 596A). There is, however, one curious passage where his answerer tentatively suggests that X is not the same in all the Xes, and Socrates rebuts the suggestion with a strange and puzzling argument. It comes in the first six pages of the *Meno*, which are the longest piece of methodology in the early dialogues; and it will be worth our while to quote it at length.

Do you think the health of a man is different from the health of a woman? Or is it the same form everywhere, so long as it is health, whether it be in a man or in anything else?—The health of a man and the health of a woman seem to me to be the same.—And so with size and strength? If a woman is strong, she will be strong with the same form and the same strength? By "the same" I mean that it makes no difference to strength as strength whether it occurs in a man or a woman. Or do you think it does?— No, I do not.—And will it make any difference to virtue as virtue whether it occurs in the young or the old, in woman or in man?—I somehow feel, Socrates, that this is not like those others.—What? Did you not say that the virtue of a man was to manage a city well, and of a woman to manage a household well?—I did.—And can one manage a city or a household or anything else well unless one manages it temperately and justly?—No, indeed. —And if they manage justly and temperately, they will be managing with justice and temperance?—Necessarily.—Then the man and the woman, if they are to be good, both need the same qualities, namely justice and temperance.—Apparently.—What about the young and the old? Could they ever become good if they were intemperate and unjust?—No, indeed.— They would have to be temperate and just?—Yes.—Then all men are good in the same way; for they all become good by obtaining the same qualities.— It seems so.—But they would not have been good in the same way, unless their virtue were the same.—No, indeed.—Since therefore the virtue of everyone is the same, try to say, & c. (*Men.* 72–73.)

In this passage Meno's reply, "I somehow feel, Socrates, that this is not like those others," gives expression to an inkling that virtue is not the same in all virtuous persons. This is the only occasion in the early dialogues where it is suggested that the term proposed for definition might be ambiguous. The suggestion is made to come from an answerer, and not from one of the most intelligent and attractive answerers in these dialogues. Socrates is represented as not entertaining it seriously for a moment; he regards it as a view natural to those who have not reflected but evidently false to those who have.

The argument which Socrates offers to convince Meno that virtue is the same in all cases apparently consists in pointing to an identity in all of them, an identity which he indicates by the words "justice and temperance." Now pointing to an identity in all the Xes does not prove that X is a univocal word unless the identity to which you point is the very thing that X means. (For example, the premiss that all tops are material objects does not prove that "top" has only one meaning, because what "top" means is certainly not "material object.") Hence Socrates' argument proves that the word "virtue" always means the same only if the thing that he points to, and that Meno admits to be present in all cases of virtue, is the very thing that the word "virtue" means. But, if Socrates can thus point to the very thing that "virtue" means, and Meno can thus instantly recognize it, why are they asking what virtue is and, according to their own account, failing to find out? They seem to know already what is the one virtue in the many virtues.

Socrates is also assuming some sort of realism as opposed to nominalism, though this again is nothing that enters his head, but only one of the logical consequences of what does enter his head. He is assuming that this form or essence or one in the many is not a word in the mouth, nor a concept in the head, but something existing in the particular Xes independently of man. Earth-mixed-with-liquid, for example, is one essence really occurring in many different things, such as fuller's earth and brickmaker's clay and so on. "In every action the holy is the same as itself, and the unholy is opposite to all the holy and like itself, and everything that is to be unholy has some one form according to its unholiness" (*Euthyph.* 5D). The identical character appears and reappears in different parts of experience, irrespective of what man may think or say.

Someone might say that, if you ask what is common to all the virtues, and expect a verbal answer, the perfect answer is "virtue," and any other word or words will necessarily be wrong. The early dialogues contain no trace of such a suggestion. Socrates' behaviour implies that there will always be some correct answer which does not contain the word "virtue" or a synonym. Now if your account of the essence of X is not to contain the word X or any synonym, it seems that it will have to consist in an explication of the structure of X, an exhibition of X in a more extended form. It will have to give X seen through a telescope, as it were, though the magnification must not be too great for the whole of X to remain in the field. Thus Socrates' behaviour further implies that X will always have a structure that can be unfolded. It will always be like the planet that becomes bigger in the telescope, and not like the star that remains a point. It will never be a simple entity having no true analysis. This implication, undetected in the early dialogues, had risen into Plato's consciousness to some extent when he wrote the *Theaetetus;* for he there conceives of a man maintaining that the primary elements have no logos, which is to say that no account can be given of their essence (201E); on this hypothesis the question What is X? would have no true answer when X was a primary element.

The foregoing discussion reveals several assumptions that must be made if Socrates' question is to be a legitimate question admitting of a true answer. First, we must assume that the word X is univocal. Second, we must assume that the thing X has an "essence." Third, we must make some sort of realist assumption about the ontological status of this "essence." And, fourth, we must assume that this "essence" is not a "primary element" but has a structure that can be explicated; for otherwise we must already know what X is in asking the question in Socrates' sense.

In view of all these assumptions, and of the possibility that we already know what X is when we raise the question, it is surprising that we are all of us so willing to ask What is X? in Socrates' sense, and so unsuspecting of the difficulties it may lead us into. One cause of our willingness seems to be the vagueness of the What-is-X? form itself. For it is, perhaps, when unsupported by a context, the vaguest of all forms of question except an inarticulate grunt. It indicates less determinately than any other the sort of information the questioner wants. The most precise form is Is X Y? since the answerer then knows that the asker wants precisely the information that X is Y or that X is not Y, whichever is true. Less precise are Where is X? and When is X?; they tell us that a time or a place is wanted, but not by reference to what we are to determine the time (whether, for example, by reference to the birth of Jesus or to a certain collision of carriages), nor how narrowly we are to define the time (for example whether to a minute or to a century). Vaguer still is Why is X? since there is an indefinite plurality of facts that are causes or reasons or explanations of any given fact. Vaguest of all is What is X? for it amounts only to saying "Please make some true statement about X." Some examples will make this clearer. Who is Abner? He is a painter. Who is Abner? He is the man who painted the portrait of Lorme in this exhibition. What is a rhombus? A thing you learn about in geometry. What is a rhombus? A plane figure. What is a rhombus? A rhomboid having two adjacent sides equal. Each of these five is a reasonable answer to a What-is-it? question; yet each is a very different kind of proposition.

The vagueness of the form of a question is usually lessened by its context. The situation in which I ask "Who is Abner?" may show clearly that I want you to tell me some relation in which Abner stands to you and no one else does, or that I want you to tell me his business. The situation in which I ask "What is potassium?" may show that I wish to know what the word "potassium" means, or whether this substance is an element, or to what class of element it belongs, or what is its atomic weight. Instead of putting the question vaguely and relying on the context to make it clear, I might do better to use a more precise form. Thus for the above four cases of "What is potassium?" I could say respectively "What does that word mean?" "Is potassium an element?" "What sort of element is it?" "What is the definition of it?"

The explanations which Socrates gives of his question provide a context determining this vague form to mean the search for essence as above described. But it is the half-felt presence of all the other possible meanings of What is X? that prevents our seeing the pitfalls in this search for essence. Whenever a difficulty arises, we interpret the question in some other way to avoid it. For example, if the conception of essence becomes momentarily embarrassing, we take What is X? as merely a request for identification. Such an evasion is always possible, because there are several other, non-Socratic senses in which What is X? is always a proper question. One of these is "What does the word X mean?," the request for a verbal definition. Another is "Give a unique designation of X," the request for a mark of identification. A third seems to be, "Make some true statement about X," for What is X? is sometimes as vague as that. The vague form What is X? is an especial temptation "to answer questions, without first discovering precisely *what* question it is which you desire to answer" (G. E. Moore, *Principia Ethica* vii).

Another cause of our willingness to ask What is X? without restriction is that it really is a useful habit to turn to definition when in perplexity. Very often, after we have pressed an inquiry a certain distance, we cannot go farther until we use more precise terms. A What-is-X? question is then in place; and, though this is always a verbal definition, the useful habit thus acquired will, in combination with our usual failure to distinguish the senses of this question, lead to our putting it in some senses and some cases where it is not useful.

Again, it often happens that a theory is put forward in the form "X is YZ," where this is supposed to be a convertible proposition; and that after some debate this theory is disproved. "X is *not* YZ." Then it is very natural to think: "Well then, what *is* X?" So we slide into the What-is-X? question without full consciousness of doing so. The *Republic* does not open with the question, What is justice?, but with the question, Is justice honesty and paying what one owes? (331C). Not until five pages later (336C), after this and another theory about justice have been refuted, is the question raised "What *is* justice?"

Lastly, we ask the What-is-X? question unrestrictedly because the following seems such a plausible argument: "If we know what a thing is, we can surely say what it is" (*La.* 190C, cf. *Chrm.* 159A). Conversely, we feel that we do not know what a thing is unless we can give some description that is convertible with it and does more than merely identify it.

# THE SIGNIFICANCE
# OF MENO'S PARADOX*

*Bernard Phillips*

Plato's *Meno* is ostensibly concerned with the ethical question, What is virtue? In the course of the dialogue, however, Plato manages to include a good deal of metaphysical and epistemological doctrine, and presents for the first time a statement of the Myth of Reminiscence. The transition from the ethical questions which are pursued in the first portion of the dialogue to the metaphysical and epistemological discussions which make up its central section seems at first reading to be rather factitious and consists of a puzzle which is advanced by Meno. The metaphysics and epistemology are then introduced by way of a reply to Meno's difficulty. Having achieved no success in his first efforts to formulate a satisfactory definition of virtue, Meno is unwilling to continue the inquiry. Socrates thereupon declares that he is as ignorant of the nature of virtue as is Meno, and exhorts the latter to take up the search yet once more. To this exhortation, Meno replies:

And how will you inquire, Socrates, into that of which you are totally ignorant? What sort of thing, among those things which you know not, will you put forth as the object of your seeking? And even if you should chance upon it, how will you ever know that it is the thing which you did not know?[1]

Socrates is evidently acquainted with the paradox, and he at once restates it in more precise terms:

I know, Meno, what you are trying to say. Just see what a specious argument you are introducing, that a man cannot inquire either about that which he knows or about that which he does not know. For he cannot inquire about what he knows, inasmuch as he already knows it and he has no need to inquire, nor can he inquire concerning that which he knows not, since then he does not know about what he is to inquire.[2]

* From *The Classical Weekly*, XLII (1948–1949), 87–91. Reprinted by permission of the author and the editor of *The Classical World*.

[1] *Meno* 80 d.
[2] *Meno* 80 d–e.

Meno's puzzle has generally, and, as I believe, erroneously been taken to represent merely a bit of typical sophistic logic-chopping. Shorey, for example, refers to it as "this eristic and lazy argument."[3] Taylor's comment on the passage is that, "At this point Meno again tries to run off on an irrelevant issue. He brings up the sophistic puzzle. . . . etc."[4] And Ritter asserts in similar vein that Meno "encumbers the investigation with the proposition advanced by the eristics, that there is no sense in looking for something which one does not already know."[5] As over against all such interpretations of Meno's paradox as irrelevant eristic, I wish to submit the thesis that the objection is perfectly germane in the context of the problem being discussed—namely the nature of ethical knowledge—and that, moreover, the entire passage is one of real philosophical import and is basic for understanding the Theory of Ideas and the related notion of Reminiscence. Far from being solely an instance of sophistic eristic, it contains in embryo one of the essential contentions of sophistic nominalism as a philosophical position, and it raises a problem which the Theory of Ideas is designed to meet, and which it must meet if it is to have any plausibility whatsoever. The seriousness with which Plato regarded the puzzle is shown by his invoking of the Myth of Reminiscence in order to reply to it. It is inconceivable that he should have gone to this length to meet an argument which he viewed as a mere sophism.

It is essential to distinguish between the import of the puzzle for Meno himself, and its significance for Plato and the wider philosophical audience which he had in mind. It is perfectly clear that the paradox is not original with Meno and that he has not thought through its implications; for him it is merely a dodge. This much is implied in Socrates' manner with Meno, and it is for that reason that Socrates warns Meno not to make of the argument an excuse for indolence:

(And hence we must not give ear to this specious argument, for it will make us idle, and is pleasing only to the slothful . . .)[6]

The paradox is evidently of sophistic origin, and though in the hands of lesser sophists and laymen it served only as a piece of verbal trick-

---

[3] Paul Shorey, *What Plato Said* (Chicago, 1933), p. 157.
[4] A. E. Taylor, *Plato* (New York, 1936), p. 137.
[5] C. Ritter, *The Essence of Plato's Philosophy* (New York, 1933), trans. by Adam Alles, p. 102.
[6] *Meno* 81 d.

ery, the argument itself expresses a philosophical point of view which is opposed fundamentally to the whole conception of the nature of knowledge and the function of reason which Plato is advancing. Socrates sees reflected in Meno's query the essential contention of the sophistic theory of knowledge, and this nominalistic empiricism, as he well realizes, must be countered, for it denies the legitimacy of the entire Socratic enterprise.

Meno's objection is not directed against the whole of human knowledge or against the cognitive enterprise as such. Meno is not expressing a general scepticism; what he questions is the possibility of achieving the sort of knowledge which they are pursuing in the dialogue. It is the Socratic type of inquiry which forms the target of Meno's paradox, and in relation to the sort of investigation which Socrates was wont to pursue, Meno's question formulates a genuine problem. For how are we to construe the question, What is virtue? Presumably it is not simply an empirical question of fact. It does not ask what is the current usage of the term "virtue"; neither does it seek to determine what any particular individual may choose to denote by the term. It is by intention an inquiry into the real inner nature of that which is designated by the conventional label "virtue"; it seeks the "essence" of virtue. The question, therefore, seems to make two presuppositions: that there is a real essence of virtue and that the human reason is endowed with the capacity to apprehend it. Both these assumptions, fundamental to Plato, are denied in the sophistic theory of knowledge as in all consistent philosophical empiricisms, and it is this denial which constitutes the tacit premise of Meno's paradox. Meno has no quarrel with ordinary questions of fact; it is only questions of the Socratic sort which from Meno's empiricist standpoint make no sense, for they presuppose a function of reason and a conception of reality which empiricism will not allow. If the question under discussion had been a merely empirical one—e.g., How many citizens are there in Athens?—then Meno's objection would have been utterly pointless, for this is a question to be answered by counting heads and not by reflection. In general, the paradox would have no relevance in connection with most of the inquiries of daily life or of science, for these may always be answered *a posteriori* by examining the facts of experience and reporting the results of one's discoveries. But the questions raised in the Platonic writings are generally not of the merely empirical variety, and they are to be answered, if at all, by some kind of rational insight or dialectic reflection and not by means of an empirical investigation. Meno's paradox expresses a fundamental doubt with respect to the possibility of such dialectic investigations, and the point of his argument is utterly misapprehended by these commentators who, like Koyré, would say that, "The objection is plausible and broad in scope. It actually implies that nothing can be learned."[7] Not merely does Meno's objection make no sense when it is interpreted as referring to all types of knowledge, but further, Socrates' reply is clearly intended to be a defense only of the particular kind of knowledge which he was pursuing. Socrates tells us in the *Phaedo* that he had abandoned the scientific type of inquiry in favor of a new kind of investigation—the search for the Idea; the Myth of Reminiscence is designed to explain the possibility of this new kind of knowledge which in some sense is *a priori*, i.e., derived from within the soul; it is in no wise an explanation of the manner in which we come by our knowledge of such empirical facts as the population of Athens. The belief that there is another kind of knowledge in addition to the empirical knowledge of the senses is a cornerstone of the Platonic philosophy, and it involves a view of the function of reason which is diametrically opposed to the sophistic conception of reason's role.

The sophistic epistemology in common with all empiricisms in the history of philosophy minimizes the role of reason in knowledge and maintains that in the last analysis it is sensation which gives content to knowledge. All seeing is held to be of the senses alone, and reason is denied any power of vision or intuitive insight. The function of reason is limited, in all empiricist philosophies, to the rearranging of the data delivered by the senses; reason from this point of view can make no material contribution to knowledge and is barred from stating any truths on its own. Meaningful propositions can do no more than refer to the data of the senses, and all knowledge is of the descriptive, factual kind. As a consequence, there can be no place for such non-empirical inquiries as ethics and metaphysics which pretend to do more than describe the brute facts, and in particular, the Socratic quest after the Idea must needs be the pursuit of a will-o'-the-wisp.

The philosophers of the non-empiricist persuasion, on the other hand, from Plato down have characteristically held out for a type or level of knowledge which is other than the empirical. They have insisted that the whole reality or being of things is not given to sensation, and they have maintained that there is a "seeing" which is not of the senses but of reason. Reason from the Platonic standpoint is not merely

---

[7] A. Koyré, *Discovering Plato* (New York, 1945), trans. by L. C. Rosenfield, p. 10.

ancillary to the senses but has its unique contribution to make to the sum of knowledge. The function of reason is to grasp the necessary in the particular; its concern is with what is valid, essential, or universal, that is with the *form* or *idea* which is the reality of the appearance. Reason can never rest content with a mere description of the facts, but seeks ever to transcend the brute givenness of things and to penetrate to their essences. This is a function of reason which is intelligible only on the assumption that reality includes an ideal dimension as well as the dimension of pure fact. Only then is there place, in addition to empirical inquiries, for inquiries of a reflective or dialectical character. Philosophy, as Plato conceived of it, is never simply a description of the actual course of fact; it always involves some kind of evaluation of the actual in the light of the ideal (i.e. the real).

It is for this reason that the Platonic tradition in the history of philosophy has waged persistent warfare against the various forms of metaphysical nominalism. Nominalism is the identification of reality with brute fact. It is the denial that the particular thing manifests any universal nature or essence to which it is pledged to conform. Nominalism cannot recognize the dialectical or reflective function of reason, since it considers all knowledge comes by way of the senses and is about particular things (as Antisthenes said, "Horses, I see; horseness I do not see"). It regards universals as merely arbitrary group-names, which, though convenient, refers to nothing that really exists. Hence, for nominalism, a definition is not, as Socrates imagined, the effort to get at the essential nature of a thing; a definition is merely a resolution to use a symbol to designate an arbitrary group of particulars. The entire Socratic enterprise is thus from the nominalist standpoint utterly incomprehensible. Such a question as the nature of virtue is perfectly meaningless. The term "virtue" is a symbol to which we may assign any meaning which we choose; we are not bound by some essence which needs to be disentangled from particulars by means of the reflective function of reason. We might properly inquire, What is the present state of linguistic usage with respect to the term "virtue"? This is an empirical question to which a definite answer is possible. Or we might ask, What particular things do we propose to designate by the term "virtue"? But to ask after the nature of virtue in and of itself is to pose an unanswerable and in fact a meaningless question. A verbal symbol either already has had a meaning assigned to it or not, that is to say, there either is a convention already prevailing with regard to the particular things which the symbol is to designate or else no such convention has as yet been established. In the former case, the meaning of the word is known and there is no call for reflection or dialectic. In the latter case, we have merely a mark to which no meaning has been assigned, and the question—What is virtue?—is on a par with the question—What is X? Meno's paradox is thus to be understood as an expression of an underlying nominalistic empiricism, and from this point of view the Socratic type of inquiry cannot be justified. If knowledge is solely about sense particulars, if reason has no power of insight into the universal essence, then in regard to any term we are in precisely the situation described by Meno—we have either agreed on the denotation of the term and know what we wish to designate by it or else we have merely a meaningless physical mark in regard to which no inquiry is possible.

Plato's answer to Meno's paradox takes the form of the Myth of Reminiscence. Actually the myth construed in anything like a literal sense does not solve the problem which is a qualitative and not a temporal one. It is not a question of when the mind came by the knowledge of the non-empirical variety, but of how it can do so, and this question is not at all illumined by the assumption of pre-existence. In each prior existence, the question may always be raised, How does the mind acquire knowledge which is not of the experimental variety? In the end one will be driven to assert what is the real point of the myth, namely, that "truth about being exists in our soul."[8] Plato is contending that the power of intellectual vision or of rational insight is as primitive in the human soul as the power of sensation is in the sense organ.[9] It belongs to the soul by its very nature. Reason is precisely the faculty which perceives the universal in the manifold of sense. The particular thing is never merely a particular; in it an essence is always enmeshed, and the apprehension of the particular simultaneously involves some apprehension, however vague, of the universal. The latter is what provides the toehold for the dialectical inquiry. Our situation is not that of being confronted with a term whose meaning has either been arbitrarily assigned or else is altogether indeterminate. We already have a more or less hazy knowledge of the meaning of the concept which we are discussing, since we have already some acquaintance with the particular instances in which it is exemplified. This vague

---

8 *Meno* 86 a–b.

9 The episode of the slave's apprehension of a geometrical truth as the result of Socrates' questioning is intended as a confirming example of the thesis that the intellect has the power of rational insight, and that knowledge is based on this power in such non-experimental fields as mathematics.

knowledge needs elucidation and sharpening, and this is the purpose of the Socratic inquiry.

What the *Meno* presents us with, therefore, is a statement of the two opposing conceptions of the nature of knowledge and of the function of reason which have formed a great divide in the history of philosophy, the one view appearing in the form of an apparently sophistical objection raised by a layman, and the other in the form of a myth. The fundamental issue raised is this one: Does the intellect "see," or is it wholly ancillary to the senses, which alone are endowed with the power of intuition? Meno's paradox is based on the sophistic premise that the power of "vision" belongs solely to the senses; the Myth of Reminiscence is the contention that the intellect as well is equipped with insight, and that the exercise of the power of vision is the proper function of reason.

# KNOWING AND SAYING: THE STRUCTURE OF PLATO'S *MENO**

*Alexander Sesonske*

Day after day, wherever men did meet in Athens, Socrates walked and mused and called them to account. Through war and peace, greatness and decline, in the midst of all his brothers he created one of the monuments of the golden age of Greece: a life whose warp was action, whose woof was speech.

If we ask, "What did Socrates do?" a simple answer comes most readily: he talked. The talk, we know, was indecisive. He persisted in shaping every conversation into a question on the nature of things. "Of course I know," his respondents would reply; and then he would teach them his great lesson—that they did not know. But Socrates did not know either; so each encounter concluded on the same note: "we have failed to discover" what courage or temperance or friendship is. A paradoxical failure; for though he could not *say* what virtue was, he displayed it daily in his actions, responding directly, correctly, courageously, temperately to the whole range of occasions and demands that comprised a citizen's life. "Of all the men of his time whom we have known, he was the wisest and justest and best." No one has been more aware of the paradox than Plato.

In Plato's early dialogues Socrates insists now and then that "of that which we know, we can also say what it is." (*Laches*, 190C) But the connection between knowing and saying transcends this simple relation. Not only can we say without knowing, but the whole Socratic enterprise assumes that saying without knowing can lead to knowledge, and suggests this, indeed, as *the* path to knowledge.

Socrates probably never formulated the problems inherent in this assumption; though he proclaimed the superiority of the examined life, it was lives that he examined and not his own procedures. The very

* From *Archiv für Philosophie*, 12 (1963), 3–13. Reprinted by permission.

circumstances of those procedures provide a reason for this. Socrates talked, he did not write; and he talked to all who would respond or listen. Thus he was condemned to repeat forever the same arguments, go through the same debate; trying each day to reassert against the failing memory of a casual and variable audience the points made but the day before. Perhaps, as Aristotle drily says, Socrates was the first to raise the problem of universal definition. But the very novelty of his problem then limited his exploration of it in the marketplace. Intellectual progress occurs only when the discoveries, or mistakes, of the moment can somehow be fixed and thus transcended. They can be fixed in writing, or in the minds of a closed discussion group, a group whose membership is constant. But Socrates' "mission" precluded both of these conditions and left him forever explaining that an example is not a definition and that yet a definition must meet the test of examples.

How many times Plato heard this explained we cannot know. But unlike his master Plato wrote the argument. Perhaps he also said, if the seventh epistle is authentic, that a man's written compositions are not his most serious pursuits. Nevertheless he devoted much of a long life to writing, and in his writings early ensnared this basic Socratic discovery and was enabled thus to hold it to account, to ask from whence it came and where it led.

It is tempting to see the *Meno* as the first accumulation point of the consequences of fixing the Socratic quest in writing. Having written aporetic dialogues and subtly explored the inconclusive give and take of a Socratic discussion, Plato could not, like Socrates, repeat again the same performance. By now he knew and had displayed the power and flexibility of Socrates' mode of argument; had shown how the innocent and the wily, the learned and the ignorant, the pompous and the humble could all be caught up in it and brought to face their inability to answer the Socratic question. But once, twice, thrice written, the lesson was clear: an example is *not* a definition; yet a definition must meet the test of examples. This need not be said again. Nor need Plato or his readers merely be reminded again that they did not know (could not knowingly say) what courage or piety or friendship is. The already written dialogues remain as constant reminders of this.

These points established, new questions must arise. An example is not a definition; but what then *is* a definition? We see that we do not know; but how then *can* we know? The written Socratic dialogue, unlike its oral predecessors, provokes us to examine the argument itself rather than the arguers. The argument in motion, the oral dialogue, keeps us engaged from point to point, intent on seeing where the discussion is going. The argument at rest, the written dialogue, allows us to see where it has been. And, having seen, ask: what is it out to do? and how can it be done?

Ask whom? Why, ask the argument; for there it is. But, alas, it cannot answer, and for this Plato proclaims it inferior to oral discourse. It cannot answer; that is, it cannot *say* anything in response to our questions. Here the paradox may come to our aid. Perhaps the Socratic argument is like Socrates, who could not *say* what virtue was, yet displayed it in his every act. The argument similarly cannot say, if asked, what its presuppositions and implications are; can it too somehow *show* them? When Socrates was asked, what is virtue? he replied, I do not know. But if beholding the life of Socrates, we ask ourselves what virtue is, we can see that to be virtuous is to be like Socrates. If the argument is asked, what underlies your questions? it preserves a solemn silence. But perhaps if, beholding the written argument, we ask ourselves what it assumes, it too may show what it cannot say. So Plato, having written, asked himself—and saw.

What he saw we may discover in the *Meno*, whose methodological digressions clearly distinguish it from the early dialogues and disclose the new cluster of questions Plato has allowed onto the stage. At the center of the cluster lies the inarticulate assumption inherent in the Socratic method; that saying without knowing will, if properly pursued, lead to knowledge. If we also accept the asserted premise, "of that which we know we can also say what it is," it follows that saying without knowing will lead to knowing *and* saying. But neither Socrates' oral disputations nor Plato's written dialogues had confirmed the assumption; they shared the common conclusion: we do not know.

In a curious way this confirms the assumption, but in a way which merely compounds the puzzle. For, most of those who spoke without knowing thought they knew, and thus spoke confidently. For them the culminating "I do not know" was indeed the attainment of knowledge. From saying without knowing they had progressed to knowing—but only to knowing that they did not know. An important step; but even if the awareness of ignorance is the beginning of knowledge, as Plato and Socrates believe, it is not the end. How can we go further?

In this context the question has a sting. The path to knowledge is through saying without knowing, but once we know that we do not know, how can we continue to say? While wrongly thinking we knew, we could sincerely say without knowing and thus progress; but now, if honest, when questioned we can only reply, I do not know. Must the process end there? If so, how can knowledge be acquired?

Still another puzzle lurks in the Socratic paradox. Though Socrates says he does not know what virtue is, he frequently suggests that virtue may be knowledge. Each attempt to prove this in discussion leads only to the same "we do not know"; nevertheless is not this assumption, too, inherent in the Socratic dialectic in which the pursuit of virtue and the pursuit of knowledge are identical? Yet, if virtue is knowledge and that which we know we can also say, what can we make of Socrates who cannot say but *is* virtuous? Perhaps the relations between knowing and saying are even more complex. Not only can and must we say without knowing if we are to know (say knowingly) but here also is a kind of knowing without saying. And this may be the key to the riddle; the problem of how saying without knowing can lead to knowledge may be resolved by seeing that quite a different kind of knowledge, a knowing without saying, underlies the dialectic.

If the "digressions" in the *Meno* are understood as Plato's response to his growing awareness of this nest of problems, I suggest that we can then see the *Meno* as a unified and comprehensible whole. The first "digression" (73E–77A) responds to a question which arises readily once Socratic dialogue has been fixed in writing. The Socratic question always has the form, "What is *x?*" But in Socrates' discussions and in the early dialogues of Plato the question was never answered successfully. This leaves us wondering, what would a correct answer be like? Supposedly, when we know we can say, but it is not at all clear just how this saying is to differ from our normal saying without knowing. Socrates had suggested some criteria for a correct definition: an example is not a definition; a definition must name what is common to all examples and only to them. Is that all? In this section of the *Meno* Plato proposes three different answers to the question, what is a definition? Each of them avoids the error of citing an example; each of them names something common to all examples. Yet they are quite different. Evidently the Socratic criteria are not sufficient.

The first example of a correct definition offered is that figure is the only thing that always accompanies color (75B). The definition meets the Socratic criteria, perhaps that is why Plato has his Socrates say that he would accept a similar definition of virtue (though we may doubt it); however it defines by mere identification of an accompanying characteristic, simply indicating a mark which distinguishes *x*, figure, from everything else, but not telling us anything at all about *x* itself.

Plato accepts the second definition, figure is the limit of solid (76A), as adequate. Here we have no mere identifying mark, but a definition by what will later be called essential characteristics. Further, the correctness of the definition is self-evident; that is, one needs only to understand the defining terms to apprehend its validity. Though the terms are used in geometry the definition is quite independent of geometric proof or theory; we need not be geometers to understand or accept it.

The third definition has none of this self-evidence or logical necessity. "Color is an effluence of figure, commensurate with sight and sensible" (76D) may be called a causal definition. Its acceptability rests upon the prior acceptance of a rather elaborate physical theory and it is subject to confirmation or refutation with the theory. In fact one may question whether the definition is even comprehensible apart from the theory. It does not enable us to identify color if we did not already know it nor cite any observable characteristics of color itself. Socrates declares it inferior to the definition of figure but does not say why.

In this first digression Plato has moved far beyond the Socratic criteria. He does not formulate new ones, but the variety of definitions tendered surely indicates an awareness of important distinctions. The question of the relation of knowing to saying cannot arise in regard to the definitions themselves; for, to function as examples, the terms Plato chooses, figure and color, must permit Socrates and Meno to both know and say without hesitation. But a different aspect of this problem plays a central role in the digression and leads toward the heart of Plato's thought.

Meno replies to Socrates' first definition, figure is the only thing which always follows color, by asking, "But if someone said he does not know what color is, any more than what figure is, what sort of answer would you have given him?" "The truth," Socrates replies; nevertheless from then on before offering another definition he carefully elicits from Meno an admission that he understands the terms to be used. The point made here is simple but fundamental: any definition requires the use of some terms which, in this context, are undefined. If the definition is to be admitted as knowledge—knowing and saying— the defining terms must be known; one must know what limit is if "figure is the limit of solid" is to provide an example of knowledge. Must we also be able to *say* what limit is—define it? And what of the terms we use in that definition?

Once seen, the necessity of undefined terms casts doubt upon the Socratic dictum, "Of that which we know we can also say what it is." If knowledge in one sense is to be constituted by definitions (knowing and saying), these themselves must rest upon a knowledge that cannot be (or at least is not) said—terms whose meanings are known but which are not defined. Of what can such knowledge consist? The answer which emerges in the later evolution of Plato's thought is, of course, that it must consist in a direct intellectual apprehension of the object of knowledge.

In the *Meno* Plato merely embarks upon the path which tends in this direction. But we may speculate about the importance of the discovery in Plato's development. If definition requires the existence of undefined terms perhaps Plato then saw that definitions of virtue also require a final reference to some term which is not defined, but whose meaning must somehow be known. How such things can be known is the subject of the second digression in the *Meno*, but beyond this we may glimpse the vision of the Good appearing on Plato's horizon.

The next section of the *Meno* (77B–80A) renews the attempt to define virtue. Thus far in the dialogue Meno has remained confident that he knew and could say what virtue was—there was merely the matter of seeing what form a definition should take. Once again, under Socrates' questioning, the terms "justice," "temperance," "piety" come into play as elements in the discourse. The familiar Socratic problem emerges: the relation of the particular virtues to virtue as a whole. But in the light of Plato's conscious concern with the nature of definition this old puzzle gains new import. Both Meno and Socrates have used the terms "justice," "temperance," etc. without hesitation, specifying them only as "parts of virtue." The preceding digression had shown that every definition requires the admission of undefined terms, but now we see that the range of terms which are admissible without definition is limited. Socrates shows Meno's latest definition to be circular and thus inadequate, but in this context a perhaps familiar logical point provokes a crisis in the Socratic quest for knowledge.

As Meno's assurance that he can say what virtue is vanishes, his confidence in Socrates also disappears. The assurance, we now see, had a fatal circularity as its basis: if asked about "virtue" Meno will use "justice," or "temperance," "honorable," or "good" as undefined terms; if asked about "justice" or "temperance" he speaks of them as "parts of virtue." As long as "justice," "honorable," etc. in one context and "virtue" in the other are admitted without definition or question,

Meno can "deliver an infinite variety of speeches about virtue." The benumbing shock now administered by Socrates consists simply in exposing the implicit circularity underlying these speeches.

Every successful definition must ultimately rest on the admission of some undefined term, but we cannot take the whole family of terms we use to talk about human conduct—virtue, honor, justice, good, noble, temperance, etc.—and admit each in turn in order to define the others. Either we must define one of them independently of all the rest and use that as the root for defining the others, or we must admit one term without definition and assign it the same key role. Meno has not done the former; rather each time a question about any of these terms occurs one of the others seems necessary in order to make it clear. And now Socrates impugns the legitimacy of the latter course. For, since these terms are so interrelated, the admission of any one of them as undefined raises the spectre of circularity. In order to know that we have escaped circularity we cannot simply *admit* a term without definition; we must *know* what the admitted term means and that its meaning does not involve any of the others. But if we know what a thing is (or what a term means) we should be able to say what it is. But then the term is no longer undefined; thus we are thrust back on the first alternative. Ultimately, for Plato, the circle will be broken by discovering a term whose meaning can be *known* even though it can't be said.

We should see now that the developing perplexity involves not simply Meno, but the whole Socratic quest. All of the early dialogues have unearthed the same circularity. Not only Meno, but all of us, when asked about virtue or justice or temperance can reply by talking of justice or goodness or virtue. Finding that Socrates forbids him from using any of these terms without definition Meno discovers that he "cannot say one word" as to what virtue is. Meno says that he cannot say; Socrates suggests that, like himself, Meno does not know, yet invites him to continue his inquiry anyway. But, feeling the impact of his own speechlessness, Meno for the first time accepts Socrates' claim of ignorance and is struck by the fact that Socrates too, if he is sincere, should be speechless.

"And how will you enquire, Socrates, into that which you do not know," he asks. "What will you put forth as the subject of enquiry? And if you find what you want, how will you ever know that this is the thing which you did not know?" (80D)

In the Socratic context, to inquire means to institute a dialectical process which begins by saying without knowing. In these terms,

Meno's questions are: once one really feels his ignorance, rather than merely professing not to know as a pedagogical device, how can he honestly *say* anything further while knowing that he does not know what he says? And if he does manage to say something, and happens to say truthfully, how can he ever tell that what he says is true? That is, how is it possible to knowingly say without knowing, and how can saying without knowing lead to knowing? As Plato sees these are crucial problems for the Socratic method.

The long digression at the center of the *Meno* (80D–86C) attempts to answer the second of these questions, how can we recognize the truth if we hit upon it? It does not directly answer the first question, how can we knowingly say without knowing; rather it urges us to do so (81D and 86C) by showing that if an inquiry can be undertaken it is possible to succeed.

If our inquiry does hit upon the truth, how can we know it is the thing we are looking for? Socrates' answer, of course, is the doctrine of anamnesis or recollection, which here comes forth as having been suggested by the notion of the immortality of the soul. The soul has learned all things and knows them, even though we cannot say what it knows; in this inarticulate knowledge in the soul lies the possibility that we may recognize the truth when we come upon it in inquiry. The analogy to empirical memory is very close and must be taken seriously if we are to understand Plato here. In memory we have a kind of knowing that cannot be immediately said; if asked about a past event I may not be able to *say* correctly what occurred but at the same time may have a memory which is *at present* inaccessible but not therefore totally unreachable. In trying to remember we engage in "inquiry" without knowing (being able to say knowingly) what we are looking for, yet we recognize it when we find it. In both cases, memory and anamnesis, the *possibility* of success rests upon a prior occurrence somehow stored within the self, the experience of the event to be remembered, the soul having learned all things. In both cases the *fact* of success remains enigmatic: when we search our memory and hit upon the correct answer we simply and immediately *know* that it is correct—we could not say how; when the Socratic inquiry reaches the "thing we are looking for" we simply know that is it—we could not say how, nor does Socrates try to explain how. But the mystery of recognition does not prevent our really remembering, and a similar inexplicability should not hinder us from inquiring.

Socrates' dialogue with the slave boy serves to illustrate the doctrine of recollection. Like Meno the slave boy does not know but

thinks that he does, thus confidently says without knowing at the out-
set. Like Meno he is reduced to silence when made aware of his own
ignorance. But he is then skillfully led by Socrates to the point of as-
serting the correct answer to the geometrical problem. When asked he
was unable to say what the answer was or even how to go about finding it, and thus did not know. Yet he could recognize as true the very
things he could not say, when they were suggested by Socrates' questions. Thus in a sense he had the knowledge in him all along as a sort of
knowing that cannot be said.

When, at the end of the sequence, Socrates suggests that the boy
still does not *know* even though he has recognized the correct answer,
we may distinguish five stages in the relation of knowing and saying
that are now clear to Plato: (1) the state of unacknowledged ignorance, when one confidently says *incorrectly* without knowing, (2) the
state of acknowledged ignorance, when one sees that he does not know
and therefore cannot say, (3) the state of true opinion which develops
in inquiry, when one confidently says *correctly* without knowing,
(4) the state of knowledge, when one knows and knowingly says, (5)
the underlying state of latent knowledge, a kind of knowing without
saying which makes the transition from state (1) to state (4) possible.

Though this complex provides an answer to Meno's second question, how is it possible for inquiry to succeed, it does not answer the
first question, how can inquiry be reinstituted after it has broken down
at stage (2), acknowledged ignorance. This problem could not arise in
the slave boy sequence. There though the slave was brought to face his
own ignorance and thus rendered speechless, Socrates was not.
Throughout the discussion Socrates has knowledge of the object of
inquiry; so when the slave is unable to say anything further Socrates
can say for him in the sequence of questions which lead him out of
ignorance. But how can *anything* be said if *all* of the parties to the
dialogue are in state (2)? This is the point which Socrates and Meno
had reached in talking of virtue. How can one honestly assert anything
while admitting that he does not know?

Plato's answer appears with the resumption of the question of
virtue at the end of the second digression. It is contained in the short
third digression (86E–87B) which introduces the concept of *hypothesis*, which we may now see as essential to the Socratic quest. For
to put forth an hypothesis is precisely to knowingly say without
knowing. We can add here another element to the growing Platonic
complex: state (2B), saying hypothetically. In the other states, (1) and
(3), in which we say without knowing, we say confidently, but state

(2) demolishes confidence to the point where we cannot say at all. Yet saying is requisite if inquiry is to continue. How can we continue? By (2B): Saying *tentatively* without knowing; saying something which we know we do not know in order to see what happens after we say it, i.e., saying hypothetically. The role of hypothesis in the problem of inquiry is similar to the role of undefined terms in the problem of the nature of definition. In each case we must start with something. In a definition we must assume a knowledge of some undefined terms. An inquiry must also start with something. If we have no acknowledged starting point we must simply choose one, hypothesize, and go on from there. If we have chosen the right hypothesis our inquiry will lead to recollection; we will acquire true opinion, perhaps even knowledge.

We can now answer what has sometimes been a puzzling question about the *Meno*. This is, why, at 87D, does Socrates speak of the doctrine that virtue is good as an hypothesis? The answer is that in this context it can be asserted in no other way. When at 80D Socrates admits for both Meno and himself that they "have no idea what virtue is" this implies that from then on neither of them can say knowingly anything about virtue. Any assertion made after this must be made tentatively, knowing that we do not know—it must be an hypothesis.

The fourth and final digression in the *Meno* is not so much a digression in the course of the argument as in its personnel. This is the encounter of Socrates and Anytus (90A–95A). Whatever political import this may have, we may see that like each of the other digressions it has a methodological point. For the third time in the *Meno* the shock of the torpedo strikes a respondent who confronts his own ignorance and is thus rendered speechless; i.e. unable to say anything in direct response to Socrates' question. However, unlike Meno who responded with a puzzle or the slave boy who submitted to further inquiry and was led out of ignorance, Anytus merely berates Socrates and walks away. But before being benumbed he had displayed yet another stage in the complex of knowing and saying.

In the slave boy sequence the introduction of "true opinion" occurs in a context of inquiry and "recollection." Stimulated by questions the boy uttered true opinions which would become knowledge if inquiry were continued and repeated. Socrates seemed there to say both that the slave has had true opinions in him all the time, and that he has reached true opinion as a result of inquiry. In the first usage true opinion refers only to the state of latent knowledge; true opinions are in us in exactly the same way that knowledge is in us (in the soul). This does not comprise a distinct stage in the complex. In the second

usage true opinion means confidently saying correctly without knowing (in the sense of really having knowledge). Here it is a distinct
phase in the growth of knowledge from ignorance, and Socrates suggests that it is a necessary step to knowledge; that is, the first time we
say truly (recollect, recognize truth) as a result of inquiry it is mere
true opinion. It has not yet been fixed by our inquiry; we are still
subject to manipulation through persuasion. As inquiry continues, as
we come to work out the reason, this true opinion becomes knowledge
and mere persuasion will no longer lead us to abandon our belief.

Anytus cannot say who the teachers of virtue are and refuses to
continue the inquiry once his ignorance is made manifest. But he does
say that the sophists do not teach virtue. Plato and Socrates agree that
this is true; Anytus says correctly. He can give no reasons for his opinion; he insists he has had absolutely no experience of the sophists. Yet
he confidently says correctly without knowing. The opinion does not
emerge from inquiry; it is simply asserted. And the discussion which
follows produces evidence to the contrary. Socrates cites the successful
life of Protagoras and the high esteem in which he was held. Thus
Anytus' view cannot be simply a matter of common public opinion,
which might be expected to shape the words, if not the views, of a
politician. In the face of such evidence Anytus should have some
strong reason for opposing a widely held view. But he can give no
reason at all. Therefore he must be inspired; his opinion is a gift of the
gods.

In this section we are not to see Socrates as a defender of the
sophists. His statement of the evidence is a necessary part of the
process of showing what inspired true opinion is. Socrates also believes
that the sophists do not teach virtue—it is a *true* opinion—but he has
had experience and can give reasons for opposing the common opinion.
And since right opinion, rather than knowledge, is a moment later to
be attributed to the historic Athenian statesmen, it is quite appropriate
that it be Anytus, the leading Athenian "statesman" at the time of the
dramatic date of the dialogue, who exemplifies this stage of the knowing and saying complex.

Anytus' assertion that the sophists do not teach virtue is an example of what Socrates at 97B calls right opinion; confidently saying
correctly without knowing and without inquiry. If anamnesis always
evolves from inquiry and results in related, systematic knowledge—
knowledge of the reason why—right opinion as displayed by Anytus
has no connection with anamnesis. Yet it is just this inexplicable saying
correctly without knowing which provides the "solution" (within the

*Meno*) of the problem, how is virtue acquired? The virtue we find in Athens is not knowledge; it is right opinion. It is neither taught nor given by nature, but a gift of the gods, inspiration.

Though this inspired right opinion is divorced from anamnesis in the *Meno*, we may still suggest that it fits well the analogy between anamnesis and ordinary memory. Often memory is a systematic recall, rebuilding a whole span of the past so that each remembered fragment reinforces the others, giving us a complete assurance of the veracity of the memory, an assurance that cannot easily be shaken without the presentation of decisive evidence. This corresponds to the Socratic recovery of knowledge by anamnesis. In contrast to this systematic recall are those occurrences of isolated fragments of memory—when we suddenly remember without trying and without a context of supporting memory. We are sometimes able to answer correctly a question about the past without knowing just where the answer came from. This resembles Plato's inspired right opinion.

The notion of inspired right opinion cannot, of course, really answer for Plato the question of how virtue is acquired; for if it were accepted it would signal the failure and the end of the whole Socratic and Platonic quest. But I may in conclusion say something about why it is a necessary outcome of the *Meno*. Here as elsewhere, I suggest, Plato uses a concept before he explains it. The introduction and explanation of "hypothesis" does not occur until we are midway through the *Meno*. But an hypothesis which is implicit in the opening line (and perhaps this helps explain why the opening is as abrupt as it is) and made explicit in the encounter with Anytus (93A) controls the whole argument of the *Meno*. The question, how is virtue acquired, is throughout the *Meno* argued upon hypothesis. The hypothesis is that there are virtuous men. If there are good men, that is, if the leading citizens of Athens *really* are virtuous, then virtue is not taught, cannot be knowledge, and is explicable only as inspired right opinion. But if there are no really virtuous men (except perhaps Socrates) none of this follows; virtue may be knowledge and be teachable (recollectable through dialectical inquiry). Plato, we may be sure, held this latter view; it was not Pericles or Themistocles who were truly virtuous men, but Socrates—and the future philosopher-kings.

A. E. Taylor, at the end of his discussion of the *Meno*, says: "The contributions of the dialogue to the theory of knowledge, the exposition of the doctrine of 'reminiscence' and the principles of method, with all their importance, are meant to be secondary . . . It would be a complete misunderstanding to find the main purport of the dialogue in these things." My interpretation is obviously at odds with Taylor's. Perhaps that is because Taylor takes the methodological discoveries to be Socratic in origin and thus subordinate to the Socratic mission; whereas I feel that they are Platonic and a major element in Plato's philosophical development.

# PHILOSOPHICAL
# DISCOVERIES*

## R. M. Hare

# I

There are two groups of philosophers in the world at present who often get across one another. I will call them respectively "analysts" and "metaphysicians," though this is strictly speaking inaccurate—for the analysts are in fact often studying the same old problems of metaphysics in their own way and with sharper tools, and the metaphysicians of an older style have no exclusive or proprietary right to the inheritance of Plato and Aristotle who started the business. Now metaphysicians often complain of analysts that, instead of doing *ontology*, studying *being qua being* (or for that matter *qua* anything else), they study only *words*. My purpose in this paper is to diagnose one (though only one) of the uneasinesses which lie at the back of this common complaint (a complaint which analysts of all kinds, and not only those of the "ordinary-language" variety, have to answer). The source of the uneasiness seems to be this: there are some things in philosophy of which we want to say that we *know* that they are so—or even that we can *discover* or *come to know* that they are so—as contrasted with merely deciding arbitrarily that they are to be so; and yet we do not seem to know that these things are so by any observation of empirical fact. I refer to such things as that an object cannot both have and not have the same quality. These things used to be described as metaphysical truths; now it is more customary, at any rate among analysts, to express them metalinguistically, for example by saying that propositions of the form "*p* and not *p*" are analytically false.

* From *Mind*, LXIX (1960), 145–162. Reprinted by permission of the editor and the author. Sections 2–5 and 7 of this paper appeared in the *Journal of Philosophy*, LIV (1957), 741, in a symposium with Professors Paul Henle and S. Körner entitled "The Nature of Analysis." The whole paper could not be printed there for reasons of space, and I am grateful to the editors of the *Journal* for permission to include in this revised version of the complete paper the extract already printed.

An analyst who says this is bound to go on to say what he means by such expressions as "analytically false"; and the account which he gives will usually be of the following general sort: to say that a proposition is analytically false is to say that it is false in virtue of the meaning or use which we give to the words used to express it, and of nothing else. But this way of speaking is not likely to mollify the metaphysician; indeed, he might be pardoned if he said that it made matters worse. For if philosophical statements are statements about how words are *actually* used by a certain set of people, then their truth will be contingent—whereas what philosophers seem to be after are necessary truths: but if they are expressions of a certain philosopher's *decision* to use words in a certain way, then it seems inappropriate to speak of our *knowing* that they are true. The first of these alternatives would seem to make the findings of philosophy contingent upon linguistic practices which might be other than they are; the second would seem to turn philosophy into the making of fiats or conventions about how a particular writer or group of writers is going to use terms—and this does not sound as if it would provide answers to the kind of questions that people used to be interested in, like "Can an object both have and not have the same quality, and if not why not?" This is why to speak about "decisions" (Henle, *op. cit.* pp. 753 ff.) or about "rules" which are "neither true nor false" (Körner, *op. cit.* pp. 760 ff.) will hardly assuage the metaphysician's legitimate anxiety, although both of these terms are likely to figure in any successful elucidation of the problem.

It is worth pointing out that this dilemma which faces the analyst derives, historically, from what used to be a principal tenet of the analytical movement in its early days—the view that all meaningful statements are either analytic (in the sense of analytically true or false) or else empirical. From this view it seems to follow that the statements of the philosopher must be either empirical or analytic; otherwise we can only call them meaningless, or else not really statements at all but some other kind of talk. Many analysts failed to see the difficulty of their position because of a confusion which it is easy to make. It is easy to suppose that the proposition that such and such another proposition is analytically true, or false (the proposition of the analyst) is itself analytic, and therefore fits readily into one of the approved categories of meaningful discourse. But, though it may *perhaps* be true, it is not *obviously* true that to say "Propositions of the form '*p* and not *p*' are analytically false" is to make an analytically true statement; for is not this a statement about how the words "and not" are used? And is it analytically true that they are used in this way? There are conflicting temptations to call the statement analytic, and empirical, and neither. The early analysts therefore ought to have felt more misgivings than most of them did feel about the status of their own activities; and this might have made them more sympathetic towards the metaphysicians, whose activities are of just the same dubious character (neither clearly empirical nor clearly analytic).

This is not to say that the matter has not been widely discussed since that time; and indeed there are certain well-known simple remedies for the perplexity. But I am not convinced that the disease is yet fully understood; and until it is, metaphysicians and analysts will remain at cross purposes. It is a pity that the early analysts, in general, tended to follow the lead, not of Wittgenstein, but of Carnap. Wittgenstein was moved by doubts on this point among others to describe his own propositions as "nonsensical" (*Tractatus*, 6.54); but Carnap wrote, "[Wittgenstein] seems to me to be inconsistent in what he does. He tells us that one cannot state philosophical propositions and that whereof one cannot speak, thereof one must be silent; and then instead of keeping silent, he writes a whole philosophical book" (*Philosophy and Logical Syntax*, p. 37), thus indicating that he did not take Wittgenstein's misgivings as seriously as he should have. At any rate, the time has surely come when metaphysicians and analysts ought to co-operate in attacking this problem, which touches them both so nearly.

Once it is realised that the propositions of the analyst are not obviously analytic, a great many other possibilities suggest themselves. Are they, for example, empirical, as Professor Braithwaite has recently affirmed?[1] Or are some of them analytic and some empirical. Or are they sometimes ambiguous, so that the writer has no clear idea which of these two things (if either) they are? Or are they, not statements at all, but resolves, stipulations or rules? Or, lastly, are they (to use an old label which has little if any explanatory force) synthetic *a priori?* These possibilities all require to be investigated.

This paper is intended to serve only as a prolegomenon to such an investigation. It takes the form of an analogy. If we could find a type of situation in which the same sort of difficulty arises, but in a much clearer and simpler form, we might shed some light on the main problem. In choosing a much simpler model, we run the risk of over-simplification; but this is a risk which has to be taken if we are to make any progress at all. If we are careful to notice the differences, as well as

---

[1] *An empiricist's view of the nature of religious belief*, p. 11.

the similarities, between the model and that of which it is a model, we shall be in less danger of misleading ourselves.

The suggestion which I am going tentatively to put forward might be described as a demythologised version of Plato's doctrine of *anamnesis*. Plato says that finding out the definition of a concept is like remembering or recalling. If this is correct, some of the difficulties of describing the process are accounted for. To remember (whether a fact, or how to do something) is not (or at any rate not obviously) to make an empirical discovery; yet it is not to make a decision either. So there may be here a way of escaping from the analyst's dilemma.

# II

Suppose that we are sitting at dinner and discussing how a certain dance is danced. Let us suppose that the dance in question is one requiring the participation of a number of people—say one of the Scottish reels. And let us suppose that we have a dispute about what happens at a particular point in the dance; and that, in order to settle it, we decide to dance the dance after dinner and find out. We have to imagine that there is among us a sufficiency of people who know, or say they know, how to dance the dance—in the sense of "know" in which one may know how to do something without being able to *say* how it is done.

When the dance reaches the disputed point everybody may dance as he thinks the dance should go; or they may all agree to dance according to the way that one party to the dispute says it should go. Whichever of these two courses they adopt, there are several things which may, in theory, happen. The first is, chaos—people bumping into one another so that it becomes impossible, as we should say, for the dance to proceed. The second is that there is no chaos, but a dance is danced which, though unchaotic, is not the dance which they were trying to dance—not, for example, the dance called "the eightsome reel." The third possibility is that the dance proceeds correctly. The difficulty is to say how we tell these three eventualities from one another, and whether the difference is empirical. It may be thought that, whether empirical or not, the difference is obvious; but I do not find it so.

It might be denied that there is any empirical difference between the first eventuality (chaos) and the second (wrong dance). For, it might be said, we could have a dance which consisted in people bumping into one another. In Michael Tippett's opera *The Midsummer*

*Marriage* the character called the He-Ancient is asked reproachfully by a modern why his dancers never dance a new dance: in reply, he says "I will show you a new dance" and immediately trips one of the dancers up, so that he falls on the ground and bruises himself. The implication of this manoeuvre is the Platonic one that innovations always lead to chaos—that there is only one right way of dancing (the one that we have learnt from our elders and betters) and that all deviations from this are just wrong. But whether or not we accept this implication, the example perhaps shows that we *could* call *any* series of movements a dance. If, however, we started to call it a dance, we should have to stop calling it chaos. The terms "dance" and "chaos" mutually exclude one another; but although we cannot call any series of movements *both* chaos *and* dance, we can call any series of movements *either* chaos *or* dance; so the problem of distinguishing dance from chaos remains.

The first and the second eventualities (chaos and wrong dance) are alike in this, that, whether or not we can say that *any* series of movements is *a* dance, we cannot say that *any* series of movements is *the* dance (*viz.* the eightsome reel) about the correct way of dancing which we were arguing. It might therefore be claimed that, although it may be difficult to say what counts as *a* dance, and thus distinguish between the first and second eventualities, we can at least distinguish easily between either of them and the third (right dance). And so we can, *in theory;* for obviously both the wrong dance, and chaos or no dance at all, are distinct from the right dance. That is to say, the terms of my classification of things that might happen make it analytic to say that these three things that might happen are different things. But all distinctions are not empirical distinctions (for example, evaluative distinctions are not); and the question is rather, How, empirically (if it is done empirically) do we tell, of these three logically distinct happenings, which has happened? And how, in particular, do we tell whether the third thing has happened (whether the dance has been danced correctly)?

# III

Let us first consider one thing that might be said. It might be said: "The dance has been danced correctly if what has been danced is the dance *called* the eightsome reel." On this suggestion, all we have to know is how the expression "eightsome reel" is used; then we shall be able to recognise whether what has been danced *is* an eightsome reel.

This seems to me to be true; but it will be obvious why I cannot rest content with this answer to the problem. For I am using the dance analogy in an attempt to elucidate the nature of the discovery called "discovering the use of words"; and therefore I obviously cannot, in solving the problems raised within the analogy, appeal to our knowledge of the use of the expression "eightsome reel." For this would not be in the least illuminating; the trouble is that we do not know whether knowing how the expression "eightsome reel" is used is knowing something empirical. We shall therefore have to go a longer way round.

It may help if we ask, What does one have to assume if one is to be sure that they have danced the right dance? Let us first introduce some restrictions into our analogy in order to make the dance-situation more like the language-situation which it is intended to illustrate. Let us suppose that the dance is a traditional one which those of the company who can dance it have all learnt in their early years; let us suppose that they cannot remember the circumstances in which they learnt the dance; nothing of their early dancing-lessons remains in their memory except: how to dance the dance. And let us further suppose that there are no books that we can consult to see if they have correctly danced the dance—or, if there are books, that they are not authoritative.

What, then, in such a situation, do we have to rely on in order to be sure that we have really established correctly what is the right way to dance the eightsome reel? Suppose that someone is detailed to put down precisely what happens in the dance that the dancers actually dance—what movements they make when. We then look at his description of the dance and, under certain conditions, say, "Well then, *that* is how the eightsome reel is danced." But what are these conditions?

We have to rely first of all upon the accuracy of the observer. We have to be sure that he has correctly put down what actually happened in the dance. And to put down correctly what one actually sees happening is, it must be admitted, empirical observation and description. But what else do we have to rely on? There are, it seems to me, at least two other requirements. As Henle correctly observes (I do not know why he thinks I would disagree) we cannot "discover the rules of a ballroom dance simply by doing it" (*op. cit.* p. 753). The first requirement is that the dance which is being danced is indeed the eightsome reel; the second is that it is being danced right. These are not the same; for one may dance the eightsome reel but dance it wrong. Though the distinction between dancing a dance and dancing it right is not essential to my argument, it is in many contexts a crucial one (and with games, even more crucial than with dances; it must, e.g., be possible to play poker but, while playing it, cheat). Even Körner, who on page 759 of his paper objects to the distinction, uses it himself on page 762, where he says, "If it [*sc.* a performance of a dance] is relevant but uncharacteristic, it is incorrect." For both these requirements, we have to rely on the *memory* of the dancers; and, as I have said, to remember something is not (or at any rate not obviously) to make an empirical discovery.

# IV

The sort of situation which I have been describing is different from the situation in which an anthropologist observes and describes the dances of a primitive tribe. This, it might be said, *is* an empirical enquiry. The anthropologist observes the behaviour of the members of the tribe, and *he* selects for study certain parts of this behaviour, namely those parts which, by reason of certain similarities, *he* classifies as dances. And within the class of dances, *he* selects certain particular patterns of behaviour and names them by names of particular dances— names which *he* (it may be arbitrarily or for purely mnemonic reasons) chooses. Here we have nothing which is not included in the characteristic activities of the empirical scientist; we have the observation of similarities in the pattern of events, and the choosing of words to mark these similarities.

In the situation which I have been discussing, however, there are elements which there could not be in a purely anthropological enquiry. If a party of anthropologists sat down to dinner before starting their study of a particular dance, they could not fall into the sort of argument that I have imagined. Nor could they fall into it *after* starting the study of the dance. This sort of argument can arise only between people who, first of all, know how to dance the dance in question or to recognise a performance of it, but secondly are unable to say how it is danced. In the case of the anthropologists the first condition is not fulfilled. This difference between the two cases brings certain consequences with it. The anthropologists could not, as the people in my example do, know *what* dance it is that they are disputing about. In my example, the disputants know that what they are disputing about is how *the eightsome reel* is danced. They are able to say this, because they have learnt to dance a certain dance, and can still dance it, and know that if they dance it it will be distinctively different from a great many other dances which, perhaps, they can also dance. The anthropologists, on the other hand, have not learnt to dance the dance which they are going to see danced after dinner; and therefore, even if they have decided to *call* the dance that they are to see danced "dance no. 23," this name is for them as yet unattached to any disposition of theirs to recognise the dance when it is danced. The anthropologists will not be able to say, when a particular point in the dance is reached, "Yes, *that's* how it goes." They will just put down what happens and add it to their records. But the people in my example, when they say "eightsome reel," are not using an arbitrary symbol for *whatever* they are going to observe; the name "eightsome reel" has for them already a determinate meaning, though they cannot as yet say what this meaning is. It is in this same way that a logician knows, before he sets out to investigate the logical properties of the concept of negation, *what* concept he is going to investigate.

The second consequence is that, when my dancers have put down in words the way a dance is danced, the words that they put down will have a peculiar character. It will not be a correct description of their remarks to say that they have just put down how a particular set of dancers danced on a particular occasion; for what has been put down is not: how a particular set of dancers *did* dance on a particular occasion, but: how *the* eightsome reel *is* danced. It is implied that if *any* dancers dance like *this* they are dancing an eightsome reel correctly. Thus what has been put down has the character of universality—one of the two positive marks of the *a priori* noted by Kant (we have already seen that what has been put down has the negative characteristic which Kant mentioned, that of not being empirical). What about the other positive mark? Is what we have put down (if we are the dancers) *necessarily* true? Is it necessarily true that the eightsome reel is danced in the way that we have put down?

What we have put down is "The eightsome reel is danced in the following manner, *viz.* . . . ." followed by a complete description of the steps and successive positions of the dancers. We may feel inclined to say that this statement is necessarily true. For, when we have danced the dance, and recognised it as an eightsome reel correctly danced, we may feel inclined to say that, if it had been danced differently, we *could* not have called it, correctly, an eightsome reel (or at any rate not a correct performance of one); and that, on the other hand, danced as it was, we could not have denied that it was an eightsome reel. The statement which we have put down seems as necessary as the statement

"A square is a rectangle with equal sides." I do not wish my meaning to be mistaken at this point. I am not maintaining that there is any temptation to say that the statement "The dance which we have just danced is an eightsome reel" is a necessary statement; for there is no more reason to call this necessary than there is in the case of any other singular statement of fact. The statement which I am saying is necessary is "The eightsome reel is danced as follows, *viz.* . . ." followed by a complete description.

We may, then, feel inclined to say that this statement, since it has all the qualifications, is an *a priori* statement. But there is also a temptation to say that it is synthetic. For consider again for a moment the situation as it was before we began to dance. Then we already knew how to dance the eightsome reel, and so for us the term "eightsome reel" had already a determinate meaning; and it would be plausible to say that, since we knew the meaning of "eightsome reel" already before we started dancing, anything that we subsequently discovered could not be something attributable to the meaning of the term "eightsome reel"; and therefore that it could not be something analytic; and therefore that it must be something synthetic. Have we not, after all, *discovered* something about how the eightsome reel is danced?

There is thus a very strong temptation to say that the statement "The eightsome reel is danced in the following way, *viz.* . . ." followed by a complete description, is, when made by people in the situation which I have described, a synthetic *a priori* statement. Perhaps this temptation ought to be resisted, for it bears a very strong resemblance to the reasons which made Kant say that "Seven plus five equals twelve" is a synthetic *a priori* statement. Yet the existence of the temptation should be noted. Certainly to call this statement "synthetic *a priori*" would be odd; for similar grounds could be given for considering all statements about how words are used as synthetic *a priori* statements. If, which I have seen no reason to believe, there is a class of synthetic *a priori* statements, it can hardly be as large as this. Probably what has to be done with the term "synthetic *a priori*" is to recognise that it has been used to cover a good many different kinds of statement, and that the reasons for applying it to them differ in the different cases. It is, in fact, an ambiguous label which does not even accurately distinguish a class of statements, let alone explain their character. What would explain this would be to understand the natures of the situations (as I said, not all of the same kind) in which we feel inclined to use the term; and this is what I am now trying, in one particular case, to do.

# V

The peculiar characteristics of the situation which I have been discussing, like the analogous characteristics of the language-situation which I am trying to illuminate, all arise from the fact (on which Professor Ryle has laid so much stress) that we can know something (e.g., how to dance the eightsome reel or use a word) without being able yet to say what we know. Professor Henle has objected to the extension of Ryle's distinction to the language-situation. "This distinction is no longer clear," he says, "when one comes to language, and it is by no means apparent that one can always know how to use a word without being able to say how it is used" (*op. cit.* p. 750). But, although I do not claim that the distinction is entirely clear in any field, in language it is perhaps clearer than elsewhere. To say how a term is used we have, normally, to *mention* the term inside quotation marks, and to *use*, in speaking of the quoted sentence or statement in which it occurs, some such logician's term as "means the same as" or "is analytic." In saying how a term is used, we do not have to use it; and therefore we may know fully how to use it in all contexts without being able to say how it is used. For example, a child may have learnt the use of "father," and use it correctly, but not be able to say how it is used because he has not learnt the use of "mean" or any equivalent expression. Henle seems to confuse being able to "decide on logical grounds" that a statement is true with being able to say "the statement is logically true." A person who did not know the use of the expression "logically true" could do the former but not the latter.

Besides noticing that the dance-situation has the characteristics which I have described, we should also be alive to certain dangers. There is first the danger of thinking that it could not have been the case that the eightsome reel was danced in some quite different way. It is, of course, a contingent fact, arising out of historical causes with which I at any rate am unacquainted, that the dance called "the eightsome reel" has the form it has and not some other form. If it had some different form, what my dancers would have learnt in their childhood would have been different, and what they would have learnt to call "the eightsome reel" would have been different too; yet the statement "the eightsome reel is danced in the following manner, etc." would have had just the same characteristics as I have mentioned (though the "etc." would stand for some different description of steps and movements).

Next, there is the danger of thinking that if *anthropologists* were observing the dance, and had been told that the dance which they were to observe was called "the eightsome reel," *they*, in reporting their observations, would be making the same kind of statement—namely a non-empirical, universally necessary statement which at the same time we are tempted to call synthetic. They would not be making this sort of statement at all, but an ordinary empirical statement to the effect that the Scots have a dance which they dance in a certain manner and call "the eightsome reel."

# VI

There is also a third thing which we must notice. If a completely explicit definition were once given of the term "eightsome reel," it would have to consist of a specification of what constitutes a correct performance of this dance. To give such a definition is to give what is often called a "rule" for the performance of the dance. Now if we already have such a definition, then statements like "The eightsome reel is danced in the following way, *viz*. . . ." followed by a specification of the steps, will be seen to be analytic, provided only that we understand "is danced" in the sense of "is correctly danced." It might therefore be said that, once the definition is given, there remains no problem—no proposition whose status defies classification. Similarly, if we were to *invent* a dance and give it explicit rules of performance, there would be no problem. But in this latter case there would be no *discovery* either. It is because, in my problem-case, we do not *start off* by having a definition, yet do start off by having a determinate meaning for the term "eightsome reel," that the puzzle arises. It is in the *passage to* the definition that the mystery creeps in—in the passage (to use Aristotle's terms) from the ἡμῖν γνώριμον to the ἁπλῶς γνώριμον.[2] What we have to start with is not a definition, but the mere ability to recognise instances of correct performances of the dance; what we have at the end is the codification in a definition of what we know. So what we have at the end is different from what we have at the beginning, and it sounds sensible to speak of our *discovering* the definition—just as those who first defined the circle as the locus of a point equidistant, etc., thought that they had discovered something about the circle, namely what later came to be called its essence. We see here how definitions came to be treated as synthetic statements; and, since the real or

[2] *Eth. Nic.* 1095 b 2; *An. Post.* 71 b 33.

essential definition (the prototype of all synthetic *a priori* statements) is one of the most characteristic constituents of metaphysical thinking, this explains a great deal about the origins of metaphysics.

Briefly, there are two statements whose status is unproblematical, both expressed in the same words. There is first the anthropologist's statement that the eightsome reel (meaning "a certain dance to which the Scots give that name") is (as a matter of observed fact) danced in a certain manner. This is a plain empirical statement. Secondly, there is the statement such as might be found in a book of dancing instructions—the statement that the eightsome reel is danced (meaning "is correctly danced") in a certain manner. This statement is analytic, since by "eightsome reel" the writer *means* "the dance which is (correctly) danced in the manner described." Should we then say that the appearance of there being a third, mysterious, metaphysical, synthetic *a priori* statement about the dance, somehow intermediate between these two, is the result merely of a confusion between them, a confusion arising easily from the fact that they are expressed in the same words? This, it seems to me, would be a mistake. For how do we *get* to the second, analytic statement? Only *via* the definition or rule; but if the definition is not a mere empirical description, then there is, on this view, nothing left for it to be but a stipulative definition, the result of a decision. So there will be no such thing as discovering how the eightsome reel is danced. There will only be something which might be described as "inventing the eightsome reel." It is preferable, therefore, to say that there is a third kind of statement, intermediate between the first and the second, which forms, as it were, the transition to the second—we settle down in the comfortable analyticity of the second only after we have discovered that this definition of the term "eightsome reel," and no other, is the one that accords with our pre-existing but unformulated idea of how the dance should be danced. And this discovery seems to be neither a mere decision, nor a mere piece of observation. But, since I am still very perplexed by this problem, I do not rule out the possibility that, were I to become clearer about it, I should see that there is no third alternative.

Before I conclude this section of my paper, and go on to describe more complicated kinds of dances which resemble talking even more closely, I have two remarks to make. The first is that, unless *some* people knew how to dance dances, anthropologists could not observe empirically how dances are danced; and that therefore there could not be empirical statements about dances unless there were at least the possibility of the kind of non-empirical statement that I have been characterising. The situation is like that with regard to moral judgments; unless *some* people make genuine evaluative moral judgments, there is no possibility of other people making what have been called "inverted commas" moral judgments, i.e., explicit or implicit descriptions of the moral judgments that the first set of people make.[3] So, if philosophical analysis resembles the description of dances in the respects to which I have drawn attention, empirical statements about the use of words cannot be made unless there is at least the possibility of these other, non-empirical statements about the use of words. This perhaps explains the odd fact that analytical enquiries seem often to start by collecting empirical data about word-uses, but to end with apparently *a priori* conclusions.[4]

The second remark is that I have nothing to say in this paper which sheds any direct light on the question (often confused with the one which I am discussing)—the question of the distinction between logic and philology. The features which I am trying to pick out are features as well of philological as of logical discoveries, and this makes them more, not less, perplexing.

# VII

I will now draw attention to some differences between the comparatively simple dance-situation which I have been discussing so far and the language-situation which is the subject of this paper. Talking is an infinitely more complex activity than dancing. It is as if there were innumerable different kinds of steps in dancing, and a dancer could choose at any moment (as is to a limited extent the case in ballroom dancing) to make any one of these steps. Talking is in this respect more like ballroom dancing than like reels—there is a variety of different things one can do, and if one's partner knows how to dance, she reacts appropriately; but to do *some* things results in treading on one's partner's toes, or bumping into other couples and such further obstacles as there may be, however well she knows how to dance. Nevertheless there are a great many things which one can do; and not all of them are laid down as permissible in rules which have been accepted before we do them. There can be innovations in dancing

---

[3] See my *Language of Morals*, pp. 124 f.

[4] See the remarks of Professor Ayer on Mr. Wollheim's valuable paper "La Philosophie Analytique et les Attitudes Politiques" in *La Philosophie Analytique*, ed. *Béra* (Cahiers de Royaumont; Editions de Minuit, forthcoming), and compare also Aristotle, *An. Post.* 100 a 7 and *Eth. Nic.* 1143 b 4.

and in speech—and some of the innovations are understood even though they are innovations.

Both dancing and talking can become forms of creative art. There are kinds of dancing and of talking in which the performer is bound by no rules except those which he cares to make up as he goes along. Some poetry is like this; and so is "creative tap-dancing" (the title of a book which once came into my hands). The most creative artists, however, are constrained to talk or dance *solo*. It is not about these highest flights of talking and dancing that I wish to speak, but about those more humdrum activities which require the co-operation of more than one person, and in which, therefore, the other people involved have to know a good deal about what sort of thing to expect one to do, and what they are expected to do in answer. It is in this sense that I am speaking of "knowing how to dance" and "knowing how to talk."

What makes co-operation possible in both these activities is that the speaker or dancer should not do things which make the other people say "We don't know what to make of this." That is to say, he must not do things which cannot be easily related to the unformulated rules of speaking or dancing which everybody knows who has learnt to perform these activities. The fact that these rules are unformulated means that to learn to formulate them is to make some sort of discovery—a discovery which, as I have said, cannot be described without qualification as an empirical one. If a person in speaking or dancing does something of which we say "We don't know what to make of this," there are only two ways of re-establishing that *rapport* between us which makes these co-operative activities possible: either he must explain to us what we *are* to make of what he has done; or else he must stop doing it and do something more orthodox. He must either teach us his new way of dancing or talking, or go on dancing or talking in our old way. I should like to emphasise that I am not against what Körner calls "replacement-analysis"; the last chapter of my *Language of Morals* is evidence of this. But we need to be very sure that we understand the functioning of the term that is being replaced before we claim that a new gadget will do the old job better.

It might be said, dancing is not like talking, because dancing is a gratuitous activity, and talking a purposeful one; therefore there are things which can go wrong in talking that cannot go wrong in dancing—things which prevent the purposes of talking being realised. This I do not wish to deny; though the existence of this difference does not mean that there are not also the similarities to which I have been draw-ing attention. And the difference is in any case not absolute. Some talking is gratuitous; and some dancing is purposeful. When dancing in a crowded ballroom, we have at least the purpose of avoiding obstacles, human and inanimate. If we imagine these obstacles multiplied, so that our dance-floor becomes more like its analogue, that elusive entity which we call "the world," dancing becomes very like talking. And all dance-floors have at least a floor and boundaries of some kind; so no kind of dancing is *completely* gratuitous; all dancers have the purpose of not impinging painfully against whatever it is limits their dance-floor (unless there are penitential dances which consist in bruising one-self against the walls—but this too, would be a purpose). And there are some markedly purposeful activities which, though not called dances, are like dances in the features to which I have drawn attention—for example, the pulling up of anchors (old style).

This analogy points to a way of thinking about our use of lan-guage which is a valuable corrective to the more orthodox representa-tional view, in which "facts," "qualities," and other dubious entities flit like untrustworthy diplomats between language and the world. We do not need these intermediaries; there are just people in given situations trying to understand one another. Logic, in one of the many senses of that word, is learning to formulate the rules that enable us to make something of what people say. Its method is to identify and describe the various sorts of things that people say (the various dances and their steps) such as predication, conjunction, disjunction, negation, count-ing, adding, promising, commanding, commending—need I ever stop? In doing this it has to rely on our knowledge, as yet unformulated, of how to do these things—things of which we may not even know the names, and which indeed may not *have* names till the logician invents them; but which are, nevertheless, distinct and waiting to be given names. Since this knowledge is knowledge of something that we have learnt, it has, as I have said, many of the characteristics of memory—though it would be incorrect, strictly speaking, to say that we *remem-ber* how to use a certain word; Plato's term "recall (ἀναμιμνήσκεσθαι)," is, perhaps, more apt. As in the case of memory however, we know, without being, in many cases, able to give further evidence, that we have got it right. And often the only test we can perform is: trying it out again. In most cases there comes a point at which we are satisfied that we have got the thing right (in the case of speaking, that we have formulated correctly what we know). Of course, the fact that we are satisfied does not show that we are not wrong; but if once satisfied, we remain satisfied until we discover, or are shown, some cause for dissatisfaction.

# VIII

Meno, in the Platonic dialogue named after him, is asked by Socrates what goodness is (a question much more closely akin than is commonly allowed to the question, How and for what purposes is the word "good" used?). Being a young man of a sophistical turn of mind, Meno says "But Socrates, how are you going to look for something, when you don't in the least know what it is? . . . Or even if you do hit upon it, how are you going to know that this is *it*, without having previous knowledge of what *it* is?"[5] In more modern terms, if we do not already know the use of the word "good" (or, in slightly less fashionable language, its analysis), how, when some account of its use (some analysis) is suggested, shall we know whether it is the correct account? Yet (as Socrates goes on to point out) if we knew already, we should not have asked the question in the first place. So philosophy either cannot begin, or cannot reach a conclusion.

It will be noticed that my dancers could be put in the same paradoxical position. If they know already how the dance is danced, what can they be arguing about? But if they do not know already, how will they know, when they have danced the dance, whether they have danced it correctly? The solution to the paradox lies in distinguishing between knowing how to dance a dance and being able to say how it is danced. Before the enquiry begins, they are able to do the former, but not the latter; after the enquiry is over they can do the latter, and they know that they are right because all along they could do the former. And it is the same with the analysis of concepts. We know how to use a certain expression, but are unable to say how it is used (λογὸν διδόναι, give an analysis or definition, formulate in words the use of the expression). Then we try to do the latter; and we know we have succeeded when we have found an analysis which is in accordance with our hitherto unformulated knowledge of how to use the word. And finding out whether it *is* in accordance involves talking (dialectic), just as finding out whether the account of the dance is right involves dancing.

Dialectic, like dancing, is typically a co-operative activity. It

[5] *Meno*, 80 d.

consists in trying out the proposed account of the use of a word by using the word in accordance with it, and seeing what happens. It is an experiment with words, though not, as we have seen, an altogether empirical experiment. In the same way, we might dance the dance according to someone's account of how it is danced, and see if we can say afterwards whether what we have danced is the dance that we were arguing about (e.g., the eightsome reel) or at least *a* dance, or whether it is no dance at all. There is no space here to give many examples of dialectic; but I will give the most famous one of all.[6] It is a destructive use of the technique, resulting in the *rejection* of a suggested analysis. An account of the use of the word "right" is being tried out which says that "right" means the same as "consisting in speaking the truth and giving back anything that one has received from anyone." The analysis is tried out by "dancing" a certain statement, *viz.* "It is always right to give a madman back his weapons which he entrusted to us when sane." But the dance has clearly gone wrong; for this statement is certainly not (as the proposed definition would make it) analytic, since to deny it, as most people would, is not to contradict oneself. So the analysis has to be rejected.

Plato was right in implying that in recognising that such a proposition is not analytic we are relying on our memories. It is an example of the perceptive genius of that great logician, that in spite of being altogether at sea concerning the *source* of our philosophical knowledge; and in spite of the fact that his use of the material mode of speech misled him as to the *status* of the analyses he was looking for—that in spite of all this he spotted the very close logical analogies between philosophical discoveries and remembering. He was wrong in supposing that we are remembering something that we learnt in a former life—just as more recent mythologists have been wrong in thinking that we are discerning the structure of some entities called "facts." What we are actually remembering is what we learnt on our mothers' knees, and cannot remember learning.

Provisionally, then, we might agree with the metaphysicians that philosophy has to contain statements which are neither empirical statements about the way words are actually used, nor yet expressions of decisions about how they are to be used; but we should refuse to infer from this that these statements are about some non-empirical order of being. The philosopher elucidates (not by mere observation) the nature of something which exists before the elucidation begins (for ex-

---

6 Adapted from *Republic*, 331 c.

ample, there is such an operation as negation before the philosopher investigates it; the philosopher no more invents negation than Aristotle made man rational). He neither creates the objects of his enquiry, nor receives them as mere data of experience; yet for all that, to say that there is such an operation as negation is no more mysterious than to say that there is such a dance as the eightsome reel. But even that is quite mysterious enough.

# Suggested Further Readings

The number of writings devoted to Plato and Socrates is enormous. We list here only a few general works and a few further works concerned specifically with the problems raised in the *Meno*. An extensive bibliography of recent writings on Plato may be found in the *Classical Weekly*, Vol. 50 (1957). In the list below, books marked with an asterisk (*) are available in paperback editions.

## DIALOGUES OF PLATO

The dialogues *Gorgias,* *Protagoras,* *Phaedo,* and *Republic* * contain further discussion of themes and problems contained in the *Meno*. The *Laches, Charmides,* and *Lysis* are good examples of the earlier dialogues which lead up to the *Meno*.

## BOOKS ABOUT PLATO'S PHILOSOPHY AND ITS BACKGROUND IN EARLIER GREEK THOUGHT

John Burnet, *Greek Philosophy; Thales to Plato* (New York, 1914).
———, *Early Greek Philosophy* * (New York, 1920).
G. C. Field, *Plato and His Contemporaries* (London, 1930).
Paul Friedlander, *Plato* * (New York, 1958).
M. A. Grube, *Plato's Thought* * (London, 1935).
Werner Jaeger, *Paideia* (New York, 1943). Vol. II contains a chapter on the *Meno*.
Richard Robinson, *Plato's Earlier Dialectic* (Oxford, 1953).
Paul Shorey, *What Plato Said* (Chicago, 1933).
J. Stenzel, *Plato's Method of Dialectic* (Oxford, 1940).
A. E. Taylor, *Socrates* * (London, 1933).
———, *Plato, the Man and His Work* * (New York, 1926).
F. J. E. Woodbridge, *The Son of Apollo* (Boston, 1929).
Edward Zeller, *Outlines of the History of Greek Philosophy* * (New York, 1931).

## WRITINGS CONCERNED SPECIFICALLY WITH THE MENO

R. E. Allen, "Anamnesis in Plato's *Meno* and *Phaedo*," *Review of Metaphysics*, XIII (1959), 165–174.

R. S. Bluck, *Plato's Meno* (Cambridge, 1961).

F. M. Cornford, *Principium Sapientiae* (Cambridge, 1952), pp. 145–161.

N. Gulley, "Plato's Theory of Recollection," *Classical Quarterly*, IV (1954), 194–213.

R. G. Hoerber, "Plato's *Meno*," *Phronesis*, 5 (1960), 78–102.

Arthur W. H. Adkins' *Merit and Responsibility* (Oxford, 1960) contains only a brief discussion of the *Meno*, but it is an excellent account of the development of Greek moral thought and Plato's role in this development, and shows clearly the historical and cultural context in which the *Meno* was written.

*NB*